AGE OF WONDERS

Player's Manual

written by
the Stratos Group

User manual produced and printed by Mars Publishing, Inc.

www.marspub.com
Edwin E. Steussy, Publisher.
Amy I. Yancey, Managing Coordinator.
Michael P. Duggan, Graphic Artist.
Lars H. Petersen, Project Editor.

Age of Wonders

Table of Contents

Contents

Player's Manual

Introduction

Somewhere to Start

In the earliest days of the world, before days mattered and were meticulously counted by short-lived things, the Elven Court ruled all living beings upon the Northern Continent, where the Wizard-king Inioch governed from the Valley of Wonders. He maintained a delicate balance of light and shadow and saw that the life of each subject in his Kingdom was not burdened by any great evil.

The principal members of Inioch's Court were a popular, yet scholarly and restrictive, society called "The Keepers." Dedicated to preserving order and maintaining peace for all the fair races in Inioch's Blessed Kingdom, they grew to considerable influence and power. The Keepers were hailed as the "Fruit of the Elves," and symbolized all that was good and right about Elven rule.

Children of Chaos

Yet for all their studies, the Keepers could not foresee the future any better than any other Seer. And so it was that they sought to shelter and nurture a fledgling race called "Humans." The Humans, extraordinarily gifted with an alien sense of ingenuity, had nevertheless been banished from their "Garden," and sought a new home. The Keepers recognized that providing the short-lived beings such a home was an ideal opportunity to expand their influence and prosper in the ways of good.

Humans were different than any other race in the land. For some races, by their nature, good came speedily and without effort, while for others, by their nature, evil threatened to plunge them into a void. For Humans, the path was not readily apparent. Unruly and restless, they possessed many savage qualities, yet some among Humankind demonstrated a great propensity for the divine. And while there were other races in the land that were neither good nor evil, the Humans were the first to seek Inioch's sanctuary.

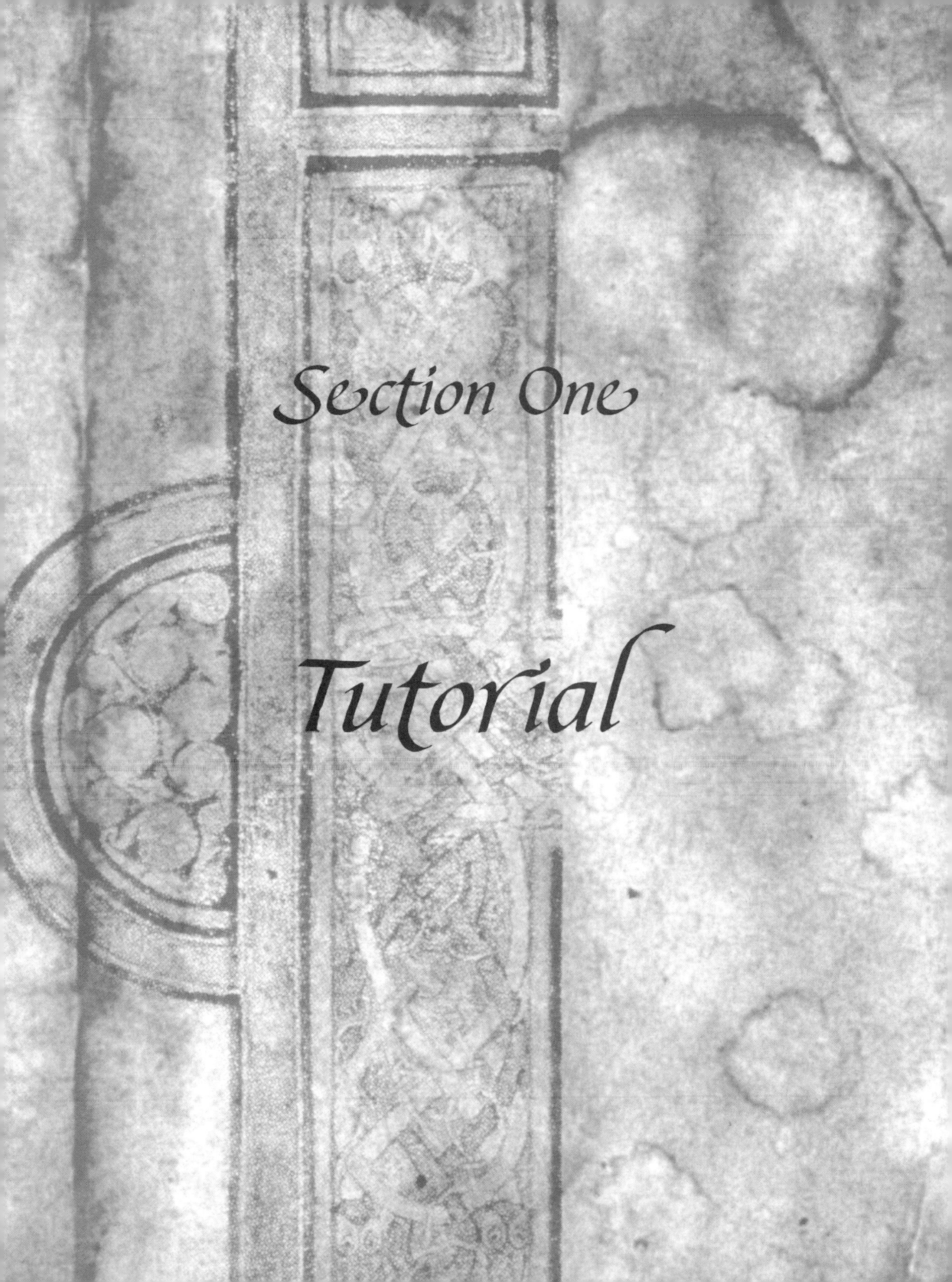

Section One

Tutorial

Tutorial

A Little About the Tutorial

The tutorial will give you some hands on experience using the *Age of Wonders* interface and teach you the fundamentals of an *Age of Wonders* game. The tutorial runs much like a simplified scenario, but instruction boxes will appear at predetermined points to guide your actions. Whenever one of the instruction boxes appears, simply read through it, hit the 'OK' button, and carry out its orders. At any time you may replay the last instruction box by hitting the F1 key. You are not bound to follow the instruction boxes exactly, but the tutorial is not designed to play like a regular *Age of Wonders* game and functions best when the instruction boxes are followed. The following sections should help you through any parts of the tutorial you may have questions about.

The Background Information Book

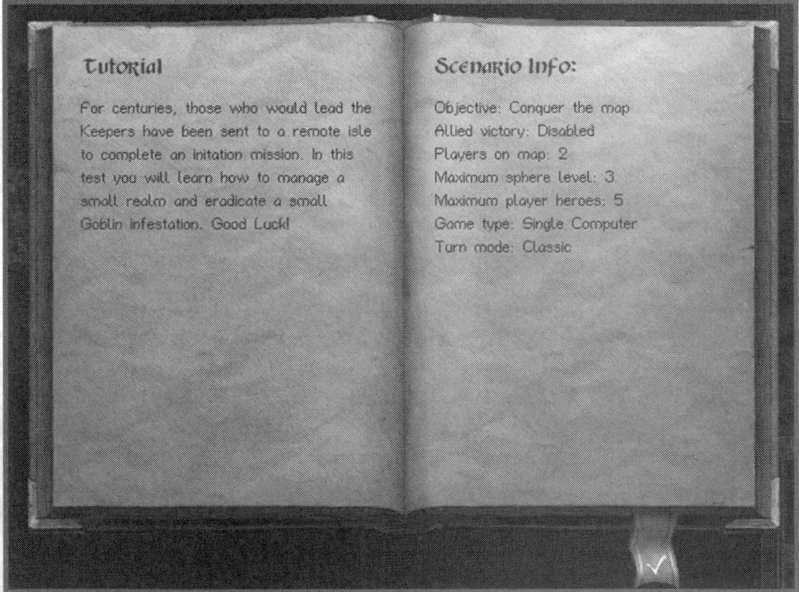

Books like this convey mission objectives and tell the story behind scenarios. The first few pages relate the story while the last page will give a rundown of the scenario options enabled/disabled. To close books like these, click on the blue check tab.

Researching a Spell

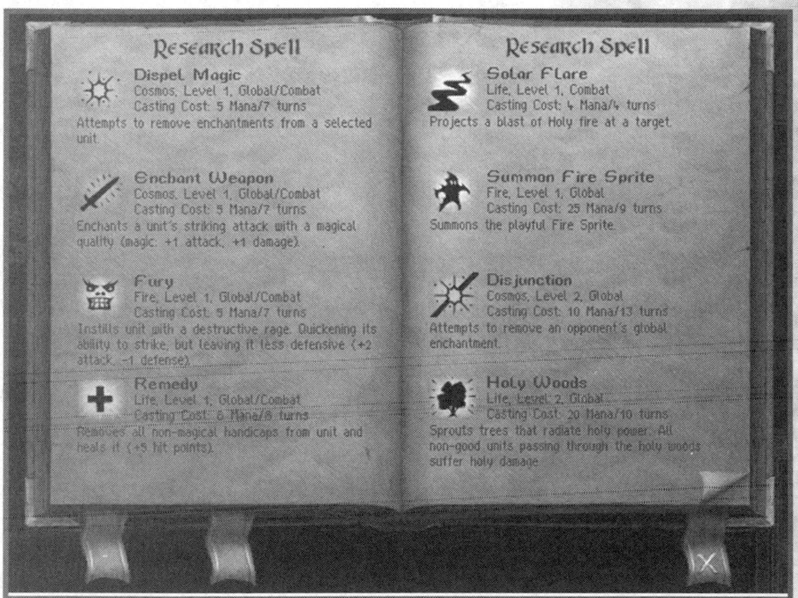

Researching a spell adds the spell to your Spellbook, allowing your Leader and Heroes to cast it. The research book provides a short description of your researchable spells. You may tab through the book using the corners at the bottom left and right of the pages.

Researching spells is rather like advancing technology. As you research more basic low level spells, more complex and useful spells will become available. The more you research in a particular sphere, the more spells in that sphere will become available to research. Long story short, research a lot of low level spells in a sphere if you wish to gain more powerful spells in that sphere later.

The Main Interface

If you need further help, you can click on the Dragon Icon in the lower left to bring up the Main Menu. The Settings menu includes a "Reset Layout" feature just in case you need to reset the windows. There is a Help setting near the bottom of the Main Menu that can provide extra information. Don't forget about the direct help feature by hitting the **?** icon when it is available on floaters.

Your Party

If you wish to deselect a unit from a party, simply left-click on the small movement icon below the unit's picture. You may also select a lone unit out of a party to move by holding a left-click on the movement icon and then right-clicking. To move units out of a Transport, like a ship, simply deselect the transport and move the rest of the units. The arrow buttons at the bottom of the party floater are used to cycle through your parties. You may take a party out of the cycle by clicking the Guard button. The Move button resumes any unfulfilled movement orders..

Out of Movement Points

Age of Wonders uses what is called a turn-based game system. Each turn, units will be allotted a certain amount of movement points, based on their speed. Faster units have more movement points and can therefore travel farther each turn. This turn base structure also applies to researching and building. One turn represents one day's worth of researching, building, and unit moving. A party will stop moving when any unit runs out of movement points. You may still move any other party members with movement points left by deselecting the exhausted units. Clicking the end turn button is somewhat akin to letting your units rest so they will be fresh to move again the next day.

City Negotiations

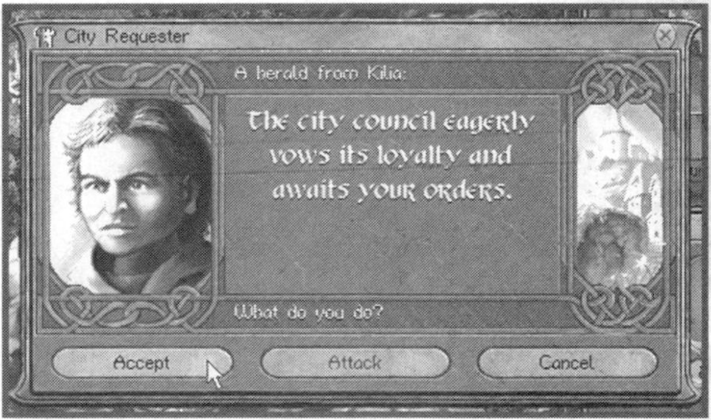

Remember for later that you don't necessarily have to accept every offer a city makes to join you peacefully. Sometimes you may want to decline a city's join offer or even attack them instead. You may not always have the gold needed to bribe a city to your side but you may still have the units to take the city by force.

The City Screen

Cities are the most strategically important resource in *Age of Wonders*. Most of your units and money will be generated from towns like this one. Size matters a great deal for cities in *Age of Wonders*. Larger cities generate more gold, can contain more units, and are capable of producing more advanced units. In general, try to control the biggest cities on the map with the largest crop fields around them. Protect your cities with walls and units and keep a sharp eye out for any neutral or hostile cities you can conquer. You will be using this screen and the City Action screen quite a bit so make sure you understand all of the functions of both screens. While it may not be obvious, your race relation with a city's population plays an important role. In general, friendly populations will help you and hostile races will revolt against you. Consider reading up on both the Town and Race Relations sections of the manual.

You may access the City screen by clicking the Enter button from the Structure floater or double left-clicking on a city hex from the Main Map.

Selecting a City Action

Get familiar with the City Action screen. Each race will have their own units to build but every town uses the same non-unit projects. There is more to the city interface than the tutorial presents and it is highly recommended you experiment, practice, and read up on how to manage your production capabilities.

A Mine

In regular games, you can claim other player's mines by moving over them in the same fashion. There are many other sites like mines that can provide income or even produce units like a city. These sites are usually not quite as valuable as cities, but some of them do provide services not available in cities. Since these sites typically require no upkeep or units to control, it is in your interest to claim as many of them as possible.

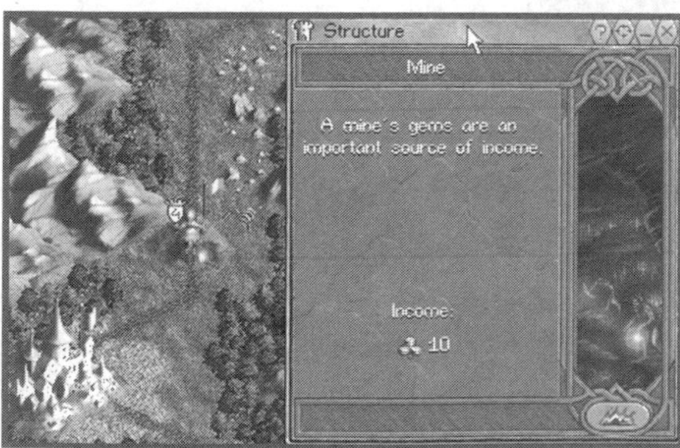

An Exploration Site

It may be tempting to explore sites like these alone with your Heroes, but the monsters in some of these sites are quite capable of devouring your units. When you encounter one of these sites outside of the tutorial, you may wish to send in a sacrificial scout unit before committing any units you can't afford to lose. For now, the monsters in the tutorial shouldn't pose much of a threat to your forces, but keep this tip in mind for later games.

Combat

When you are about to enter combat, you are given a choice between Automatic Combat and Tactical Combat.

Automatic combat is usually used as a time saving device. Minor battles don't really require you to use tactical combat to insure victory. In most cases when your Heroes or Leader is involved in a fight, it is advisable to take the tactical mode unless the fight will be easily won. Be careful about engaging very destructive units like the suicidal Goblin Bombers in automatic combat if there are specific units in your army you wish to make sure come out alive or unscathed.

A Cave

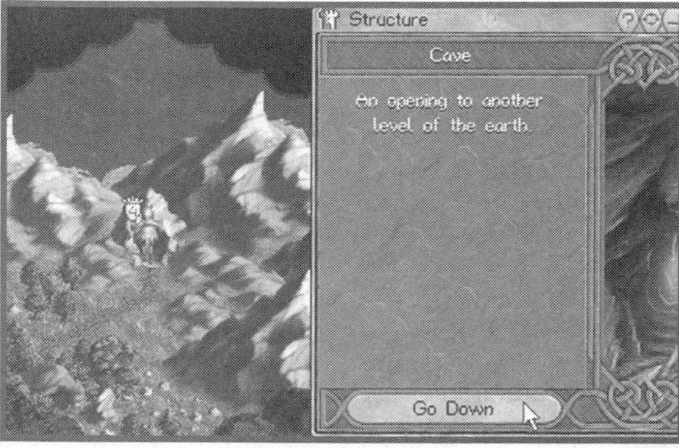

These caves represent serious strategic points. Many cave dwelling races can quickly traverse to any point on the map through the caverns below the mainland. Controlling the surface does not guarantee your enemies are not advancing on you from below.

Press the Go Down button on the Structure Window in the lower-right corner to enter the caverns below.

A Power Node

Magic Power drawn from Power Nodes can be channeled to either generate Mana Crystals (for casting spells), or Spell Research. Leader and Hero units have the Spell Casting ability that allows them to cast spells both inside and outside of combat.

Magical spells have a great variety of uses in *Age of Wonders*, from simple feats like shooting flaming arrows at your enemy, to more complex feats like causing an earthquake under a city! To use a spell outside of combat, click on a Hero's unit icon in the Party floater and hit his Spell Casting ability. Inside of tactical combat, you can use the Spell Casting ability just like any other unit ability. (You will read more about tactical combat ability usage later on in the tutorial.) Using the Spell Casting ability brings up a book much like the research book listing all the spells you may currently cast.

Some spells last forever, like enchanting a unit's weapon, but expend several mana crystals each turn, while others are used up instantly and require only the initial investment of mana. Not all spells are immediately cast when you click on their entry in the book. The level of the Hero or Leader's Spell Casting ability determines how much mana they channel into spells each turn. In short, more mana expensive spells take longer to cast, and the higher your Hero/Leader's Spell Casting ability, the less time spells take to cast. An important note for later is that since tactical combat does not span multiple turns, if your Hero does not have the ability to cast the spell immediately, it is impossible to cast the spell during combat! It won't help your empire much to have an immensely powerful combat spell if your leader or heroes can cast it.

A Wizards' Tower

A Wizards' Tower will offer a spell for sale, so you won't have to research it. In most cases, buy the spell if you can afford it. In the long run this will allow you to pump more of your power base into stockpiling mana crystals and less into research.

Making Some Friends

Don't ever turn down free units if you can avoid it. Do be careful about letting units join that you can't afford to upkeep.

Tactical Combat

The tactical combat interface is handled much in the same way as movement is handled in the main map window. Only those units with the Strike ability can engage in melee combat. Units with Strike can be ordered to attack by simply telling them to move onto their target.

Units like Centaurs capable of both melee and ranged attacks will default to melee strikes if you direct them to move onto an enemy.

Don't forget that you must manually select a ranged attack to make it work. The red circle represents the maximum range of your attack. Any unit on the edge or inside the red circle can be targeted. Be careful about firing a missile attack at an enemy too close to your units or walls. When a circle appears on a unit or object in your ranged attack's flight path, the number in the circle represents the chance that you'll accidentally hit that target instead! You can hurt or even kill your own units by accidentally firing into them. An important exception to this rule is when a unit is standing directly behind another unit or structure. You may fire through any unit or structure immediately in front of you with no chance of accidentally hitting the target. This makes cover an important part of ranged offense and defense and lets your melee units work well when paired next to archers.

Have the Giants break down the enemy walls by hurling boulders at them. After the walls are broken through, you can still hurl boulders at the enemy units!

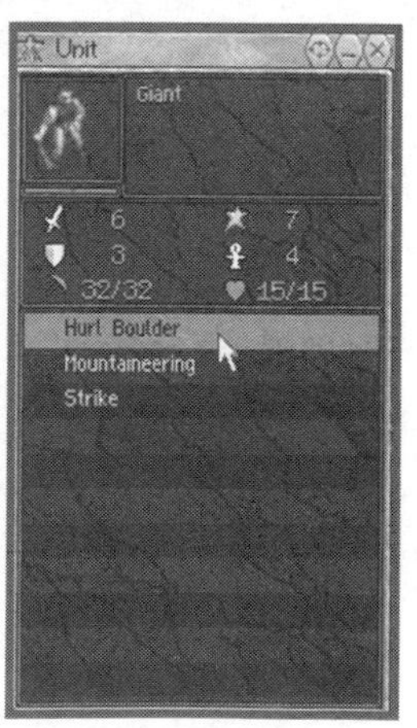

What to do With an Angry Populace?

Improving relations with a hostile race is a slow and difficult process, but if you do not eventually make peace with a race, you may be forced to fight them to the death! It is up to you to decide for each race whether peace or war is better. Most of the time it's easier to migrate in a new population to a city rather than looting or razing it to the ground. Large cities are hard to come by and should never be destroyed unless you have no intention of holding the city. Use good judgment in the future when deciding which cities are worth holding and which will serve you better as firewood. Looting and razing generates a lot of hostility, so avoid destroying cities filled with an ally's race.

A Teleporter

Like caves, teleporters can offer quick movement across vast stretches of land. Keep an eye out for units trying to make sneak attacks through the teleporters and be prepared to use them for your own purposes. Be very careful with teleporters, some teleporters do not function in both directions! Sending your units through an unexplored teleporter may trap them far away from your cities or even launch them straight into the clutches of the enemy! Use caution and exploring units when dealing with teleporters.

The Final Battle

When you are fighting an enemy Leader or Hero in a battle, try to take him out first. Slaying a race's Leader puts an immediate end to their empire and frees up your units to pillage and conquer their remaining scattered cities. High-level Heroes and Leaders are sometimes capable of making devastating spell and ability attacks and should be terminated as soon as possible.

Section Two

Getting Started

AGE OF WONDERS

Main Menu

AGE OF WONDERS
Version: 0.65.0136
Scenario
Campaign
Tutorial
Load Game
Exit

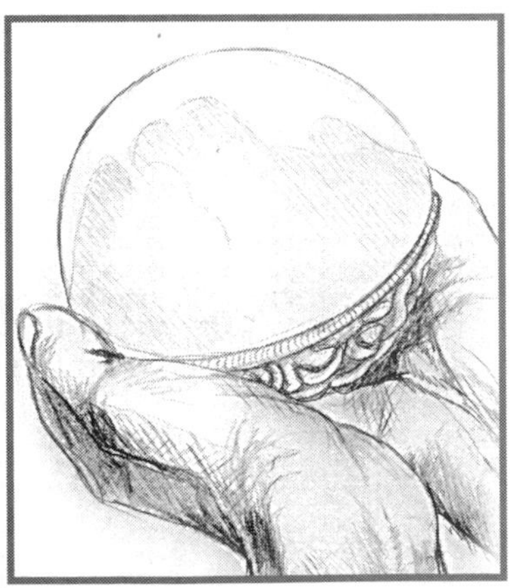

Title Screen

Welcome to the *Age of Wonders* title screen. From here you will be able to access the different *Age of Wonders* game styles.

Scenario

A scenario is a single *Age of Wonders* game played on one map. Each scenario stands alone; no continuous plot or faction is developed between scenarios (although many of the included Scenarios are part of the overall tale of the Valley of Wonders). Scenarios typically offer some customization and often support a varied choice of starting races. All multiplayer games are considered to be scenarios.

Campaign

A campaign is a series of related scenarios. You may choose between two different factions to serve, the Keepers of the Faith or the Cult of Storms. Each faction will play out a different campaign but will develop the same storyline as the two vie for control of the Valley of Wonders. No matter which path you choose, you will be presented with many choices during the course of the scenario, and you'll have to make some judgement calls as to the direction your faction will follow. Between missions, you will have the opportunity to determine which of your troops continue on with you.

Tutorial

The tutorial is a short scenario specially designed to teach the basic interface and controls used in *Age of Wonders*. It is recommended you try the tutorial even if you are familiar with games similar to *Age of Wonders*.

Load Game

Select this button if you have a previously saved game of *Age of Wonders* that you would like to load. You will be prompted to select the directory location of your saved games and which saved game in the directory to load. The information displayed across the bottom from left to right is: number of players, map size, number of cities, and turns already played.

Exit

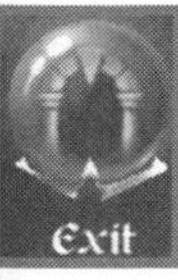

Eventually, you will need to leave *Age of Wonders*. When the time comes to leave the game, click on the exit button to return to your operating system.

Scenario Screen Information

Single Computer

Games played on a single computer allow for either one player versus up to eleven computer players, or Hot-Seat play between human players. Hot Seat games must use the 'Classic' Turns style (Page 22).

Tcp Internet

When you are connected to the Internet (usually via your Internet service provider), you can play a scenario with other people online. You may use a mix of human and computer controlled opponents in Internet scenarios.

Ipx Lan

IPX LAN scenarios work like TCP Internet scenarios with the exception that you need to be connected to a local area network instead of the Internet to play with other humans.

Play by E-mail

In an E-mail game, each human player takes a turn and then sends the scenario's saved game file to the next human player in an E-mail file attachment. Play by E-mail games require Internet access AND access to an SMTP (Simple Mail Transport Protocol) mail server. The Simultaneous Turns style, as well as tactical combat, is not available in Play by E-mail games.

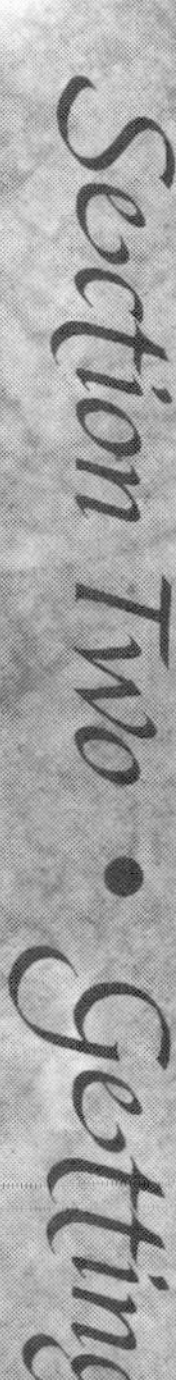

Heat.NET

HEAT.NET is a free Internet based gaming community. HEAT.NET makes it easy to locate other *Age of Wonders* players and allows for easy setup of TCP Internet scenarios.

Back to Title

If you decide not to play a scenario, hit the Back to Title button to return to the *Age of Wonders* title screen.

Setting up Scenarios

Selecting a Map

The first selection to make when starting a new scenario is to choose a map. Maps vary in size, terrain layout, number or players, playable races, and number of cities. When the "Select a Map" window appears, scroll through the list and select a map that interests you. Across the bottom of the window are displayed three icons. The letter next to the globe icon indicates the size of the selected map: XL for extra large, L for large, M for medium, and S for small. The small town icon represents the total number (not type or size) of cities on the map. Finally, the human head icon represents the total number of races on the map, but not necessarily the number of races available for play.

Once you've selected a map, hit the "Select" button and the "Select a Map" window will disappear, revealing the main scenario screen. Each of the playable races will now be highlighted, and underneath its name will be one or two fields. If the first field designates a human player or an independent, there will be no second field. If the first field designates a computer player, a second field will be visible. You may modify the owner of the race with the first field. In single computer scenarios, you must turn on Classic Turn Style to allow for more than one human player.

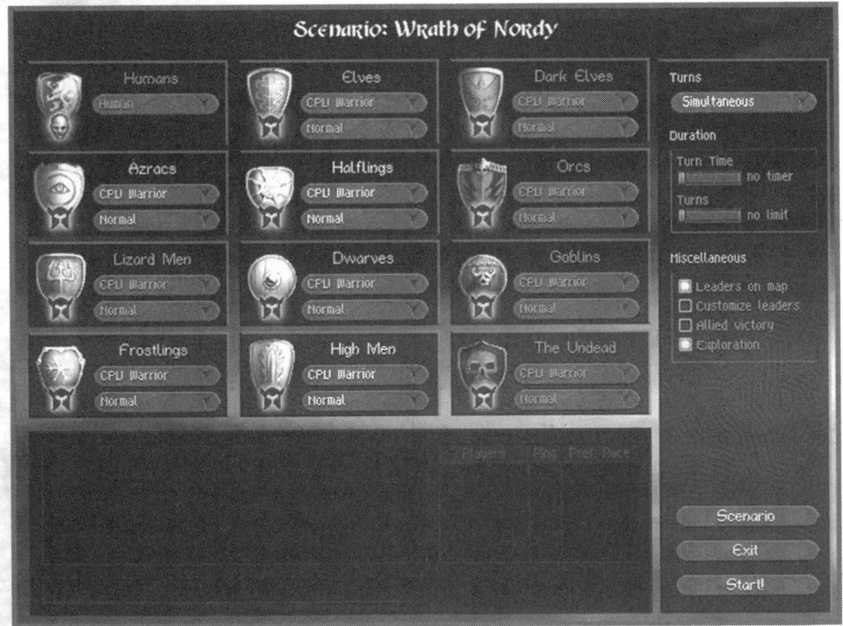

The Races

A rundown of each race is available in the Race Descriptions section of this manual.

Player Settings - Top Field

This field allows you to customize the owner of a faction.

Human – A human player.

CPU Squire – The easiest AI setting.

CPU Knight – The medium difficulty setting.

CPU Lord – The most difficult AI setting.

Independent – Setting a faction to independent changes the faction to a neutral third party Leader. Independent cities will not function cooperatively with each other, but will still defend and patrol their territory.

AI Behavior Setting - Bottom Field

Apart from the choice of level difficulty, you can customize the behavior of the computer players to better simulate a real player.

Normal – An attempt to imitate the "normal" play style of a human opponent, borrowing a little from each of the other behavior settings.

Aggressor – The computer will constantly seek out new cities to conquer and will take a more hostile response to most situations. Aggressor AI's will likely be in a constant state of war with one or more factions.

Defender – Defense will be the main concern of the computer player. It will fortify and upgrade its cities to offer them the maximum amount of protection.

Expander – Expanders love to, well, expand! They will seek out any available cities, mines, nodes, etc. to take over. Although not necessarily an openly hostile race, they will turn to warring on other factions if they are running low on alternatives.

Scorcher – The most xenophobic AI setting. The computer runs rampant and seeks not to conquer its enemies, but to butcher them and burn their cities to the ground.

Random – A behavior profile is randomly chosen and will not be revealed to the human players.

Player's Manual

Game Play settings:

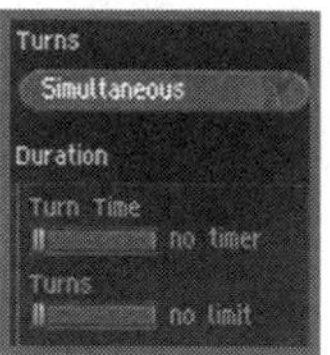

Turns

Classic – The standard turn-based model. Each player moves units and performs other necessary actions while the other players' factions remain fixed. Each player will play one turn at a time until every player has had a turn and the cycle begins anew. Classic turns allows you to play multiplayer, Hot Seat games on a single computer.

Simultaneous – Similar to the classic turn-based model, but each player takes his or her turn at the same time. Once a player is finished with their turn, they click the end turn box, and wait for the other players to click the end turn box as well. A very important thing to note is that UNITS MOVE IN REAL TIME under this setting, while all other functions are handled in the classic turn-based style. After all players have clicked in to end the current turn, the next turn begins.

Duration

Turn Time – This allows you to limit the amount of real time a player has to finish their turn. The default setting allows for an unlimited amount of real time to pass while playing a turn, but you may scale this limit from one to twenty minutes.

Turns – The total amount of turns the scenario will last. The default is an unlimited number of turns, but you may limit the total turns from 10 to 400.

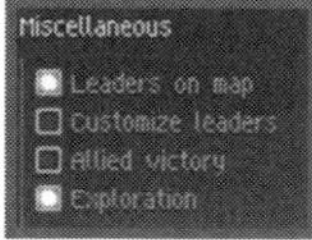

Miscellaneous

Leaders on Map – When highlighted, each race begins with their respective Leader as a Hero-type unit. Leaders are powerful and useful additions to an army, but should the Leader be killed in combat, your faction will be utterly defeated.

Customize Leaders – You are allowed to custom tailor your Leader to your preferences using the Hero leveling system. If the Leaders on Map selection is not highlighted, you may still customize the Leader and his magical spheres, but it will not actually appear as a unit in the game.

Allied Victory – Turned on, this allows for multiple factions to claim victory in a scenario. Whenever a nation wins the scenario, all factions currently allied with them also achieve victory. When not selected, only one faction will ever be able to win the scenario.

Exploration – Toggles the need to explore the blacked out portions of the map. When this option is selected, players will need to use units or spells to reveal map terrain.

Changing the Map

If you wish to change the map again, hit the scenario button to bring the "Select a Map" screen back.

Starting and Exiting

Once you have set the scenario up to your liking, hit the Start button to begin the game.

If you wish to exit back to the Game Type screen, hit the Exit button.

Multiplayer Differences

TCP and IPX multiplayer games use the same general interface as a single computer game, with a few additions.

Chatting

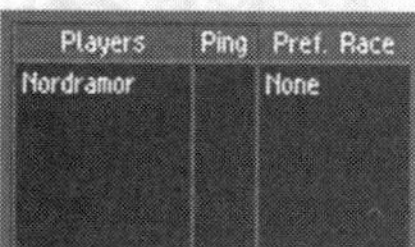

TCP and IPX multiplayer games support a small chat box beneath the race selection box. Type a message in the small box, hit enter, and it will be sent to all other players in the game and displayed in the larger box.

The Player Information Box

The player information box tells you the name, ping, and preferred race for each player currently connected to the game. The ping number represents the amount of time it takes to transfer information between the player's computer and the game host. The game will only run as fast as the slowest person's ping. The preferred race feature allows a player to pre-select which race they would like to play if the map allows it. A player will automatically be assigned his preferred race if the spot is available, but may still change it later. You may modify your preferred race in the field above the "Scenario" button.

Section Three

Leaders

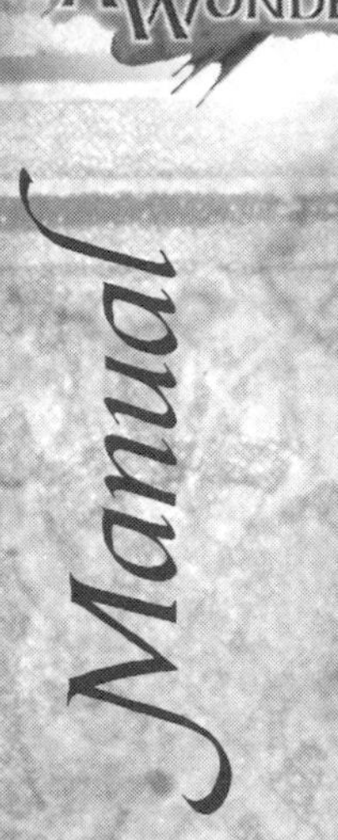

Debate and Consequences

Inioch's Court bubbled with debate, but ultimately the Keepers prevailed, and the Humans were given a place within the kingdom to settle, with the stipulation that the Humans would be strictly monitored. Should they disrupt the good balance of the rich kingdom, or if they ignored the edicts of the kingdom, they were to be removed.

Five years later, Inioch was slain. The court lay in ruins. The bodies of the fallen Elves were callously heaped into a mountain of dead and left to rot. Soon thereafter, Humans drove all the remaining Elves, and any other non-Human, from the Valley of Wonders, claiming it as their new home.

The Rise of Vengeance

Devastated by the assault upon his father's Court, mistaken for dead, and eventually heaped with the corpses of his fallen friends, Meandor, first-born son of Inioch, limped from the Valley of Wonders, beaten and abused. Though he would heal physically, his soul remained scarred and red with anger. He could hear nothing but the song of vengeance. He gathered his allies into the shadow of his torment. Dark Elves, who had long grown their forbidden colonies in secret, deep within the black earth, joined him. They demanded that the world heed Meandor's call for vengeance, no matter the cost to Elven life or soul. And so a new political party was born from the ashes of Inioch's Court. So zealous in its goals was the faction, that even its followers considered it a religion, and named themselves the "Cult of Storms."

The Cult employed any means necessary to inflict havoc upon the usurping Human race, which held the Valley of Wonders and grew steadily in power. War poured over the earth. Still the Humans grew and persisted and found ways to survive, as if inspired by the afflictions they suffered at the hands of the cruelest of torturers.

Customizing Leaders

Age of Wonders allows you to customize your Leader at the beginning of most Scenario games.

Before you customize your Leader, you must enable the "Customize Leaders" button located on the right hand of the Scenario screen.

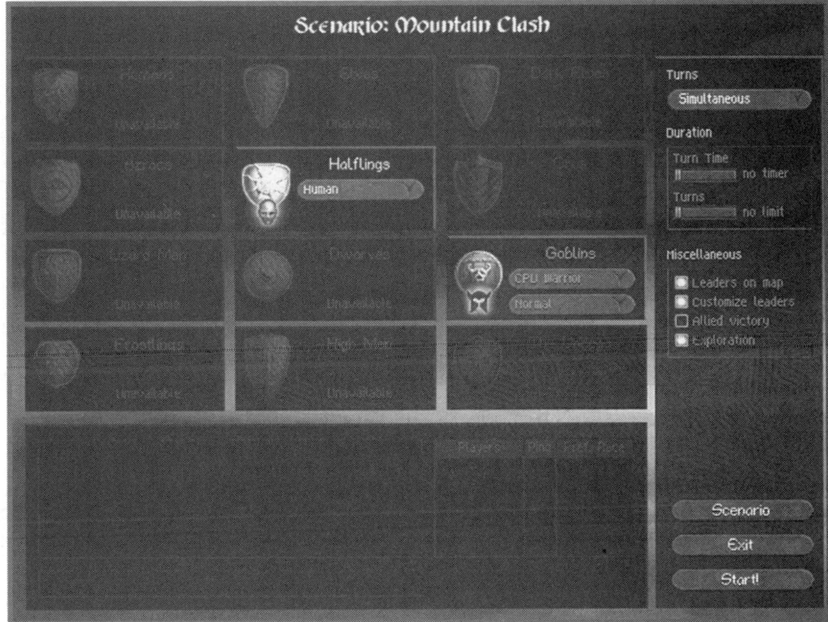

Once you have enabled "Customize Leaders" and have chosen the desired options on the Scenario screen, click the "Next" button.

Step 1: Customize Leader

After you have clicked the next button, a screen entitled "Step 1: Customize Leader" will appear. This screen is shown below.

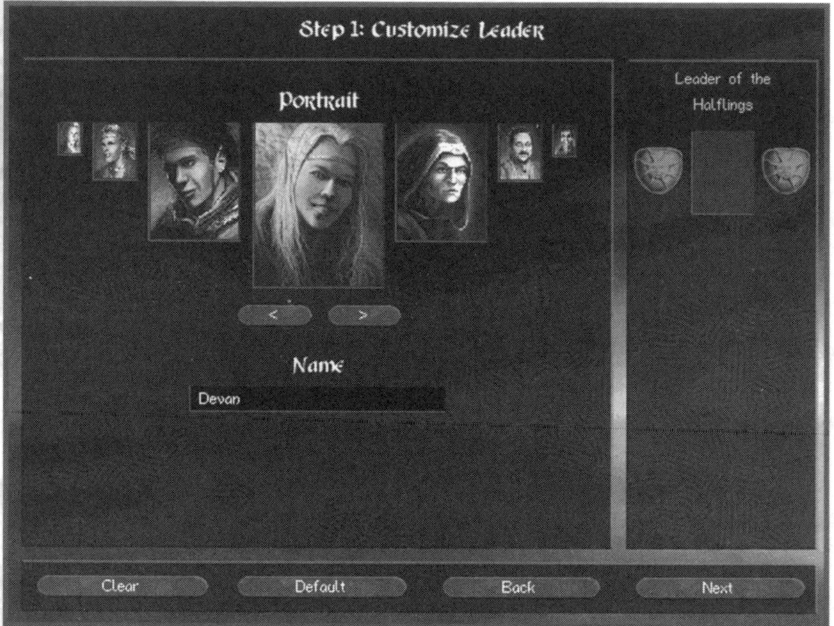

This screen allows you to select a portrait and name for your Leader. While this does not offer you any strategic advantage, it can be rather nice to add a personal touch to your Leader during a skirmish or online game. Take note that even if you choose a different race for the portrait of your Leader, your Leader's race will still be the same race you selected to play on the Scenario menu.

Step 2: Assign Skill Points

The 2nd step after you have chosen the name and picture of your Hero is to select their abilities and bonuses. This takes place on the "Step 2: Assign Skill Points" screen shown below.

Most Leaders start out without any skill points available to spend, so you must sell current abilities and statistical bonuses to obtain skill points. You can sell abilities by clicking on an ability on the left, under "Leader Abilities," and selecting remove. You may sell statistical bonuses by clicking on the down arrow next to the final column under "Leader Statistics" beside the desired statistic. Once this is completed, you should have a few skill points to re-distribute as you see fit, adding abilities from the "Available Abilities" menu, and increasing statistics. Once you are finished, select "Next" from the selection of buttons below.

Step 3: Assign Spheres

The 3rd step involves selecting the spheres of magic that your Leader will employ during the course of the game. The "Step 3: Assign Spheres" screen lets you make the appropriate choices, and is shown below.

Referencing the Magic System section (Page 83) will give you tips about how to select the best combination of spheres of magic. While there is a STRONG advantage to selecting the maximum amount of one sphere, and then whatever else is available, it can also be advantageous to select an even variety of spheres.

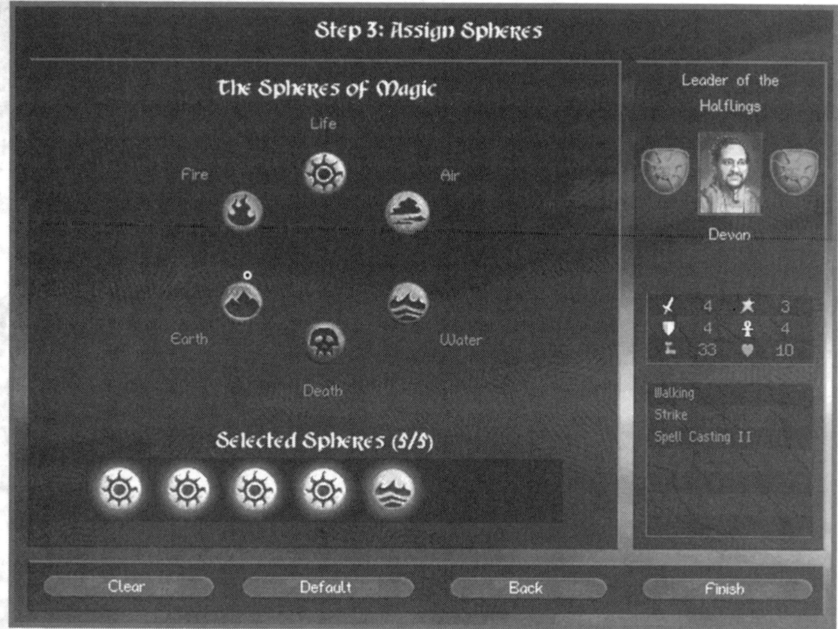

Advantages

There can be many advantages to the abilities, statistical bonuses, and magical spheres that you select, but they tend to vary from playing style to playing style. For instance, if you tend to rely upon brute strength, it might benefit you most to sell off all of your abilities in trade for statistical bonuses of defense, attack, and damage. However, if you play with more finesse and rely upon special abilities, it might be beneficial to trade in some statistical bonuses for special abilities. Be wary of using your Leader in battle however, as he is meant primarily to be a spell caster, and should only enter battle when absolutely necessary. Lose your Leader, and it's game over.

Section Four

Campaign Selection

Campaign Selection

Pick a Campaign

Before you start a new campaign, you must first select a faction to serve. Each faction has a separate campaign, but they both develop the same story. Click on the portrait of a faction to see a brief description of its goals.

The Keepers

- Preserve harmony over the Earth and its inhabitants.
- Accept humans and their presence.
- Actively oppose the Cult of Storms.
- Avoid bloodshed and conflict when possible.

The Cult of Storms

- Rid the world of both Humans and Keepers.
- Rebuild the Elven Court in the Valley of Storms.
- Resurrect the greatest Elven Lord, Inioch.
- Restore order under their own law and power.

Once you have clicked on a faction, you may either confirm your decision by hitting the Join button or re-select by clicking the Back button.

Determine your Leader

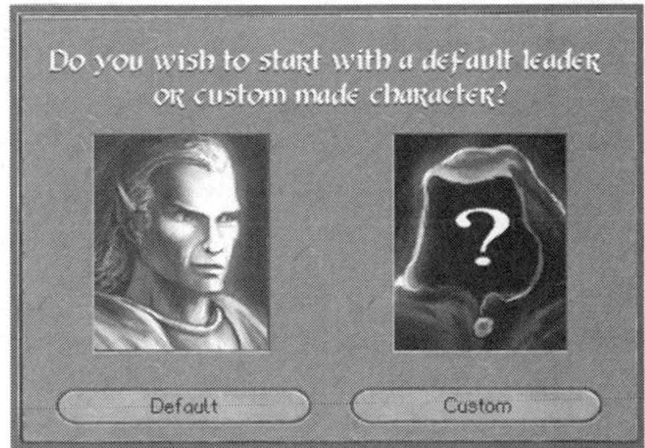

Once you have read the short campaign intro story for your faction, you will be presented with the option to start with the default Leader or to create your own. If you wish to create your own, you will need to be familiar with the Leader creation system (Page 27).

The Background Story

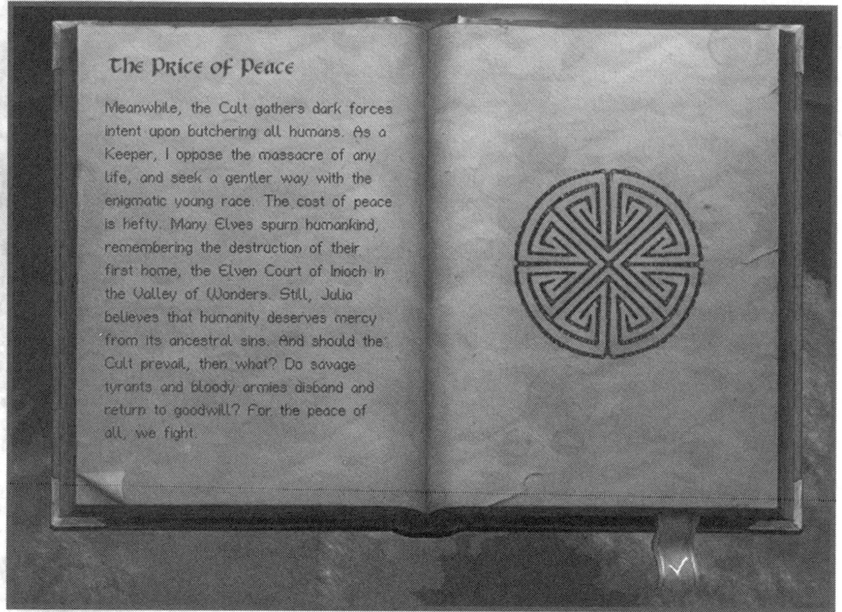

Once your Leader selection is made, you will be taken to the main campaign map. A book with the background behind your Leader's goals will appear. Scroll through the story by clicking on the page tabs on the bottom-right or bottom-left of each book page. Once you have finished reading the story, clicking on the blue check-mark tab will close the book.

The Main Campaign Map

Once the book has disappeared, you will be presented with several options from the main campaign map.

Select a Destination

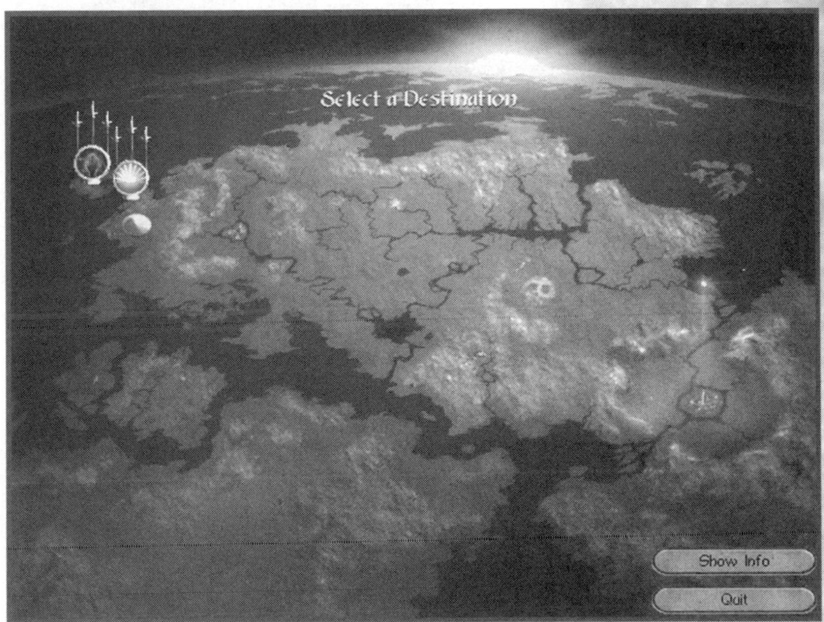

To select a mission to begin, click on the destination icon. The book again will reappear with the mission description and goals. Scroll through the pages, and when you're ready to begin the mission, click the blue checkmark You may return to the main campaign map by clicking on the red X tab.

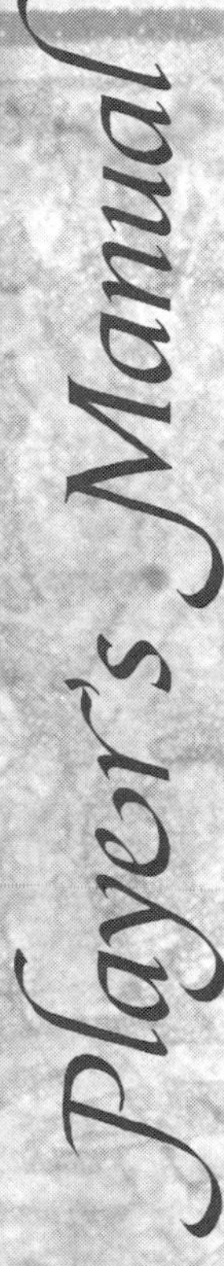

Show Info

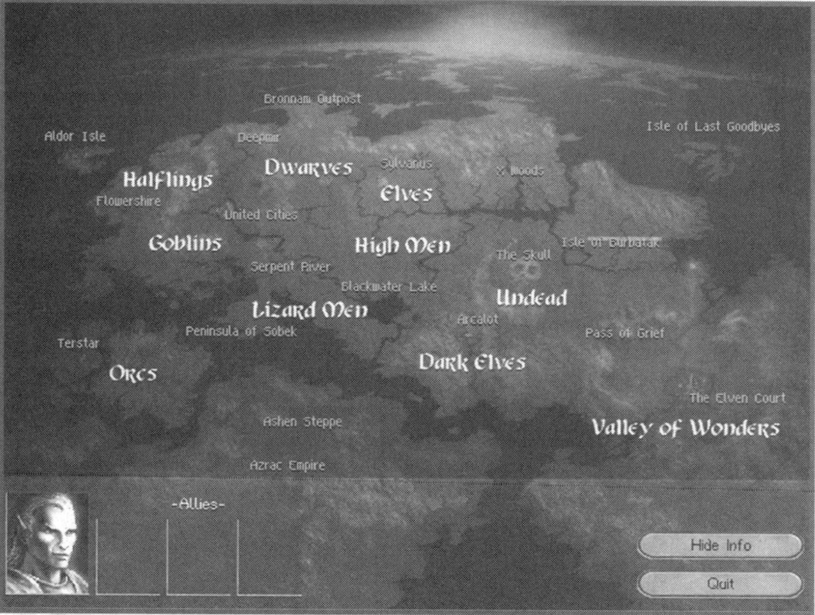

The show info option changes the map into a dissection of the various races and the lands they inhabit. A list of the races allied with yours will have their Leader's icon displayed on the bottom-left of the screen. To return the main map to normal, click the Hide Info box.

Quit

If you decide not to play the campaign any further, click on the Quit button to return to the title screen.

Section Five

Game Interface

Main Game Interface

General Use of the Age of Wonders Interface

Age of Wonders allows you to customize the game interface. The only unchangeable aspects of the interface are the preset bars, icons, and buttons located in the Bottom Menu. The Main Map can be resized to your liking, but must exist on at least a portion of the screen. Most other windows appear in what are called 'floaters' and can be moved, resized, or removed. Most of the floaters use a simple control system located in the top bar. You may move a floater by holding down the left mouse button on the top bar and dragging the floater around. If a minus sign is present on the top bar, clicking on it will reduce the floater to a small bar in the Bottom Menu.

If an X is present in the top bar of the floater, clicking upon it will remove the floater, but it will not leave a bar in the Bottom Menu. If a circular icon, similar to the mouse cursor when selecting objects, is available in the top bar, you may click on it to center the main map window upon the unit, town or event the floater is describing. Finally, if a question mark is present in the floater's top bar, clicking it will reveal the in-game help information about the floater. If at anytime you wish to remove a floater without clicking on the X icon, you may right-click to remove the floater. The events and world map floaters cannot be removed with the default right-click command however; you must manually click upon the minus icon to minimize them.

Main Map

The main map window is located on the left-hand side of the screen by default. This is the main interface window for controlling your race in *Age of Wonders*. You may scroll the window by moving the mouse cursor to the edge of the screen in the direction you wish to scroll. Whenever an object under the cursor is selectable, a circular icon with 4 arrows will appear. If multiple selectable objects are present on the same square, multiple clicks will systematically page through each one. The best example of this is when units are present on a town square. The first click will bring up the party floater, the second click will bring up the structure floater, and a third will skip back to the party floater. If you wish to immediately enter a town from the Main Map, double left-click on one of the town's hex locations.

When a party is selected, the cursor changes to a movement cursor. You may plot the path of your units by left-clicking the movement cursor on your desired destination. The party will automatically plot the shortest route toward the destination with a series of path arrows. The arrows displayed in yellow indicate how far the party can travel in the current turn. Any path arrows displayed in gray will require more turns to reach. Your final destination will be marked with an X, and if it will require multiple turns to reach, it will have the number of extra turns of movement needed displayed above it. To order your units to follow the path, simply click on the destination again or hit the Move button. No more than 8 units may exist in any given hex. Transports may not exist together in the same hex and limit the unit max in the same hex to their capacity. Not all transports allow 7 other units to exist in the same hex.

If your destination lies on an enemy unit or town, the icon will change to reflect your possible actions. An icon with two crossed swords means a battle will occur when the units meet. If two faces appear instead, it means diplomatic negotiation is possible, but not necessary. Should you engage an enemy unit in combat, you will be prompted to choose either tactical or quick combat. Tactical combat is played out on a special sub screen using a turn based combat system. Quick combat is resolved by letting the computer quickly resolve the combat based upon the units' statistics. If you approach a unit or town and engage in diplomatic relations with them, you will often be given the chance to buy them to your side with gold. If you do not wish to pay the fee, you may opt to decline this offer and leave peacefully, or go into combat.

Bottom Menu

The Bottom Menu is not customizable like floaters and the Main Map. The Dragon (Main Menu) icon appears to the far left. The preset bars across the bottom are the World Map, Realm, Magic, Relations, and Events bar. If you have minimized any other floaters, like the Structure floater, an appropriately named bar will appear to the right of the Events bar. Beneath the bars lie the Message bar, Player and Time icons, the Gold icon, and the Mana icons. Finally, on the far right, the Next Unit and End Turn buttons are displayed.

The Dragon Icon

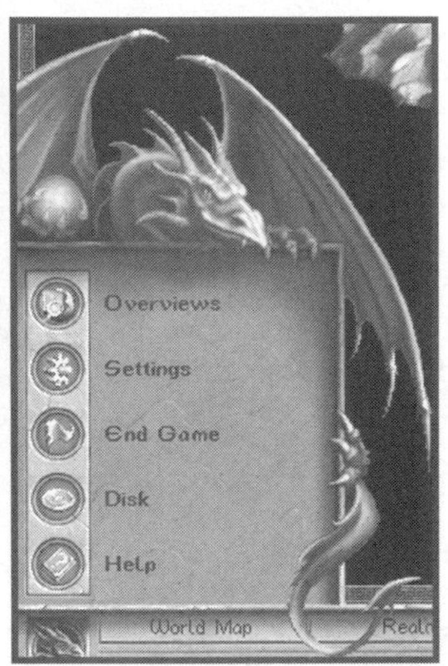

The dragon that dwells in the bottom menu bar watches over some of the most important functions in *Age of Wonders*. Clicking on the dragon brings up the Menu Menu, which functions as a series of sliding menus instead of a floater. Slide the cursor to a topic, and then follow the name out to the right to expand the menu. To close the Main Menu, right-click anywhere on the Main Map.

Overview – Lets you re-read the Background surrounding your current scenario.

Settings – From here you may access the various environmental controls: Display, Sound, Gameplay, Reset Layout, and E-mail. Display allows you to alter the game's resolution. The Sound menu controls the volume of *Age of Wonders*' sounds and music. You may edit the music play list for the map from the Sound menu. Gameplay lets you turn on the auto save feature, turn on faster movement animations, and opt to skip the *Age of Wonders* intro. You may also password protect your game and pre-select your mode of combat from the Gameplay menu. The Reset Layout feature restores the interface to the default configuration. Lastly, the E-mail setting is used to configure your mail server information for play by E-mail games.

End Game – Surrendering ends the current battle and shows you the scoreboard. You may bypass the scoreboard and go straight back to the title screen by selecting Exit to Title. The last option, Exit to Windows, exits *Age of Wonders* completely.

Disk – Save Game stores the current game file to disk. Load Game allows you to choose a previously saved game and play it from the saved point.

Help – Brings up a selection of helpful information topics to choose from.

World Map

The World Map bar brings up the World Map floater, which functions as your mini-map. The World Map floater remains on the Main Map by default and may only be minimized with the minus icon. You may change the display between the Surface, Cavern, and Depths layer by clicking on the desired layer's name. Not all maps include a Cavern or Depths layer. There are three toggle displays on the right side of the World Map floater.

Town Toggle – The topmost toggle toggles on/off the display of cities.
Unit Toggle – The middle toggle toggles on/off the display of units.
Structure Toggle – The bottom toggle toggles on/off the display of non-city structures, such as mines.

Clicking on a location anywhere on the World Map centers the Main Map on that location. The white rectangle shown on the World Map indicates the portion currently being shown on the Main Map. You may quickly scroll the Main Map by clicking and holding the mouse button and dragging the white rectangle to any spot on the World Map.

Realm

The Realm bar summons the Realm Overview floater. The Realm Overview floater is actually a menu of several sub-menus. You may alternate between the sub-menus using the four tabs at the top. You must minimize the floater with the minus icon.

Gold – Provides a breakdown of your entire empire's expenses and incomes. Your current gold stockpile and net income are listed on the left. The middle field is a comprehensive breakdown of all your daily income-generating sources. The rightmost field details all of your daily gold expenses.

Realm Overview

GOLD | CITIES | PLACES | HEROES

City Name	Population	Inc	Lvl	Wal	Siz	Rel	Mor	Act	Enc
Tansifar	Orcs	36	1	-	3			-	-
Uineth	Orcs	21	1	-	1			-	-

Cities – Provides the basic information on your cities in a short spreadsheet. The first category lists the city's name. The second, Inc, displays the city's gross income. Next is displayed the Upgrade level of the town. The Wall category shows whether the town has a wooden wall, stone wall, or no wall. The Size category shows the exact map size of the city. Relationship displays a face that mimics your race relation with the city's inhabitants. Morale displays a face image of the population's morale. An icon displayed beneath the Act category indicates the city's action if it is engaged in any activity other than Producing Merchandise. The final category, Enc, shows if the city is currently under any magical enchantments. Clicking on a category title will sort the cities by that category. You may center the Main Map on a city by double clicking on its entry in the sub-menu.

Places – Keeps track of all non-town structures currently under the control of your empire. Structure types are listed in the left field, and their activities are listed in the right field. You may center the Main Map on a place by double clicking on its entry in either field.

Realm Overview

GOLD | CITIES | PLACES | HEROES

Hero Name	Health	Level
Nordramor	15/15	3

Info

Heroes – Each Hero will be listed by his name, followed by his current health/maximum health, and his level. When an entry is highlighted, the Hero's portrait will be displayed on the left, and you may bring up his unit information by clicking on the info button underneath the portrait. Double left clicking on an entry will center the Main Map on the Hero.

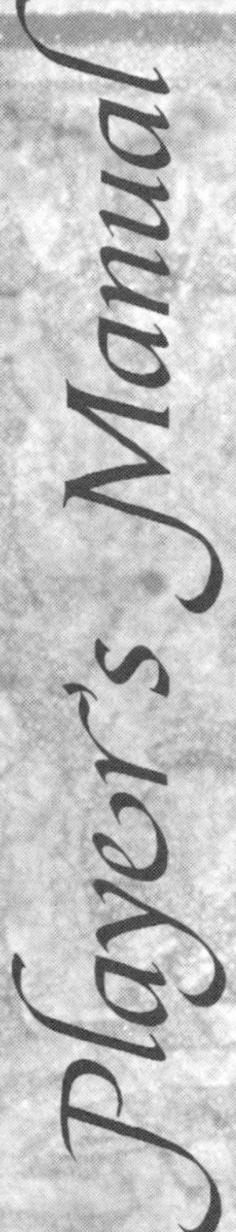

Magic

Clicking here brings up the Magic Management floater menu. Like the Realm floater, it makes use of sub-menus. You may alternate between the sub-menus using the four tabs at the top. You must minimize the floater with the minus icon.

Main – Displays the basic information on your mana management. Power Base is the raw income of mana you receive each turn. From your Power Base, your points are split between Research and Mana Income. If you wish to assign more or less of your Power Base to Research or Mana Income, use the Power Distribution button to modify the amount being put into each. The spell you are currently researching is displayed in the right field with its name and picture. Beneath its name is listed the spell's magical sphere, spell level, mana casting cost, and the current turns remaining to finish researching it. If you wish to change the spell you are researching, click on the Research button.

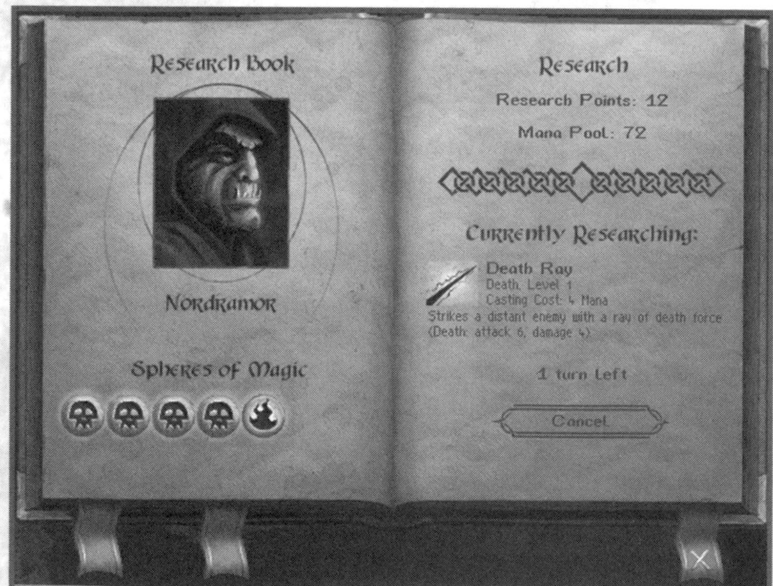

Magic Management

MAIN | SPELLS | GLOBAL | POWER

Enchantment	Binding	Mana Upkeep
Summoned	Fire Sprite	3

Spells – The first field, Enchantment, shows the types of any spells you are currently supporting. The second field, Bindings, shows to what the spell is bound. The final field, Mana Upkeep, displays the daily mana cost the spell requires to stay in effect.

Magic Management

MAIN | SPELLS | GLOBAL | POWER

Global Enchantment	Owner	Mana Upkeep
Enchanted Roads	Nordramor	10

Global – The first field shows the name of any global spells in effect. The second field shows the owner of that spell. The third field shows any daily mana upkeep needed to maintain the spell.

Power – Pinpoints exactly what is generating mana for your empire. The source of the power is listed in the first field, and the amount it generates per turn is listed in the second. You may double-click on a source to center the Main Map on the source, if possible.

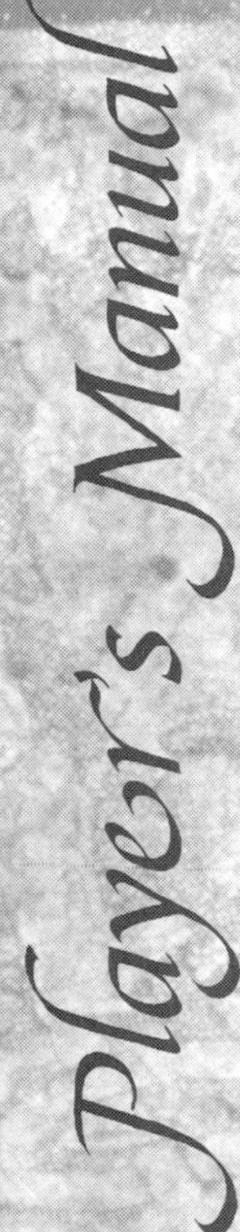

Relations

Clicking here brings up the Relations menu. This special menu does not function as a normal floater. For more information, consult the Race Relations and Diplomacy section of the manual (Page 67). To close the Relations menu, click on the Exit button in the bottom right. You will not be able to make use of any other window while the Relations menu is up. In case a combat occurs, you will automatically be pulled from the menu.

Events

The Events floater keeps you up-to-date on any significant developments and records a history of your turns. Your Leader's information, banner, and icon will be displayed at the top, along with the number of turns passed. You may bring up your Leader's unit information by clicking on his portrait. Below the portrait is the Event History list, which automatically records all significant events your race witnesses or participates in. Certain recorded events can be replayed from the event history by double clicking on their entry. Like the World Map, the Events floater remains on the Main Map by default, but may be minimized with the minus icon. The centering icon in the top bar of the Events floater centers the Main Map on your Leader.

Message Bar

The long message bar will display any useful system messages from the computer.

Player and Time Icon

Depending on what turn options are enabled, this icon serves different functions.

Simultaneous – Each race that has finished their turn will have a small box highlighted beneath their color in the turn status area.

Classic – Only the active race will have the box beneath its color highlighted. The order of the gems represents the player's turn order.

Limited Turn Time – Displays your time remaining for this turn.

Unlimited Turn Time – The clock represents the Windows system time.

Gold and Mana Icons

The three gold piles indicate the gold icon; the blue crystal indicates the mana icon. The first number indicates your current gold or mana stockpile. A green plus sign before the second number indicates the following amount will be added to your gold/mana reserve at the end of the turn. A red minus sign indicates the following amount will be subtracted from your gold/mana reserve at the end of the turn.

Next Unit

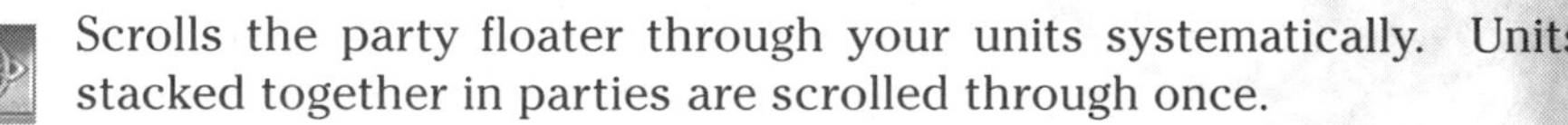

Scrolls the party floater through your units systematically. Units stacked together in parties are scrolled through once.

End Turn

Depending on the turn style, the end turn button acts differently.

Simultaneous – You may select and deselect the end turn button as long as you are not the last player to finish the turn. You may move your units after you have selected the end turn button, but unless you deselect the end turn button, the turn will end abruptly when the last race ends their turn.

Classic – Ends your race's turn and releases all control to the next race.

Party Floater

The party floater appears whenever you select a unit, and all units currently stacked in the same square are displayed. A maximum of 8 units are allowed in one square and on the party floater at one time. If you wish to bring up information on a unit, click the unit's portrait. Special unit abilities, like spell casting, are handled from the unit description screen. An alternative is to right-click on the unit portrait to bring up a simplified banner with the unit's statistics and abilities. To view data on unit abilities, right-click on the ability from the unit information screen. The selected party's movement points and its movement type are displayed beneath the portraits. The party's morale status is displayed to the right of the party movement box. Unlike the events or world map floater, the party floater may be removed by right clicking anywhere on the main map window, as closing the party window will deselect the current party. The centering icon will center the main window map on the party.

All units capable of movement are selected when you click on a party, but you may deselect units by clicking on the movement icon below their picture. Holding the left mouse button and pressing the right button on the movement icon will deselect all but the selected unit. Units may board a transport by moving onto the same hex as the transport. To remove units from a transport, deselect the transport and move the rest of the units off.

The two arrow buttons on the bottom menu allow you to page forward and back through your parties. To remove a party from the cycling pattern, click on the Guard button. Guard mode affects all units in the hex and remains on until you manually turn it off. Finally, if your units ran out of movement points while moving toward a destination on a previous turn, hitting the Move button will resume their movement along the path.

Structure Floater

The structure floater covers a wide variety of important sites, ranging from cities to mines to nodes. The typical structure floater tells the structure's name, displays its portrait, tells what its purpose is, and what, if anything, it is producing. Each structure floater typically has a raze icon, resembling a fire, located beneath its portrait, which allows you to destroy the structure if sufficient units are present. Certain non-town structures also allow you to enter them and set up production lines much like a town. To access the production screen of a structure, click on the enter button. The centering icon for the structure floater centers the main map window on the structure. The structure floater behaves the same as the party window in removing,minimizing, and relocating.

Section Six

Structures

The Rise of Sacrifice

Humiliated by their terrible failures among the Humans, the few Keepers that remained kept their allegiance quiet. Popular opinion held that the Keepers sought to destroy the Court to grab power for themselves. Many Keepers were stoned and their libraries burned, as the Elves tried to do something to appease the hurt in their hearts.

Only Queen Elwyn, Inioch's second wife, believed the Keepers' credo that the Humans could turn to the ways of peace and good. Having escaped the slaughter in Inioch's Court—bringing along her newborn daughter, Julia—she witnessed the sacrifice of the bravest Keeper Heroes. Elwyn knew the popular opinions were false, and so, she defiantly protected the fragments of the group that remained, though it cost her potential subjects. As soon as she could find shelter for her refuge-seeking followers, she set to helping the Keepers accomplish their mission.

For the next two centuries, the Keepers slowly worked to rebuild their hopes for a peaceful co-existence with humanity. Most races viewed the Keepers with suspicion, but the fair races of the surfaces feared Meandor for the dark scars upon his soul and his fearsome allies. Using Elwyn's meager resources, the Keepers made every effort to counter the damage done by the Cult of Storms. Elf slew Dark Elf; Dark Elf slew Elf in bitter battle.

Towns

Towns are the most strategically valuable resource in *Age of Wonders*. Towns produce many of your units and typically serve as your main source of income. The differences between towns lie in the following factors.

Population

Each town in *Age of Wonders* is inhabitable by only one race at a time. Different races use different units, and react differently to your empire, based upon their race relations with you. Some populations will be friendly toward your empire and may even offer to help. However, a population composed of hostile race will not serve your empire well, and may even rebel against your rule.

Size

Size represents a relative measure of the population and how much land it encompasses. Towns come in four sizes, numbering from one to four. The smallest towns are size one and take up one hex on the Main Map. The largest towns are size four and take up four hexes on the Main Map. The larger the town, the more units can defend it, the more income it generates, and the more it can be upgraded. A size three town is strategically more valuable than three size one towns.

Upgrade Level

The upgrade level of a town represents its relative technological advancement. Upgrade levels range in value from one to four, with one being the lowest and four being the highest. Towns cannot exceed their size in upgrade level, so size one towns cannot be upgraded. Upgrades increase the income a town generates and allow for the construction of superior units.

Walls

Walls represent the most basic form of defense for towns. There are two types of walls, weaker wood walls and stronger stone walls. Not all towns initially possess walls, but every town can have wood or stone walls built. Enemy ground units attempting to conquer a town must break through the walls before they can enter the city. Most normal units cannot destroy walls; special siege weapons are required. Battering Rams are the most basic unit capable of destroying walls using their Wall Crushing ability, but some other siege weapons and some spells can destroy them as well.

Town Interface

Towns and the Structure Floater

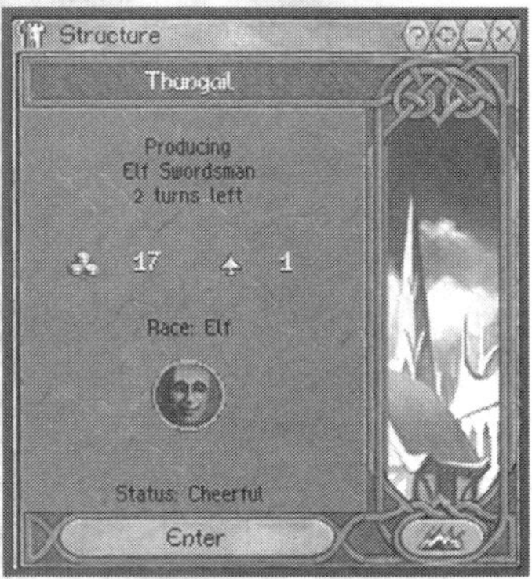

Towns are rather unique structures and have several extra fields of information in the floater. On the floater, towns list what they are producing, how long it will take them to produce it, their current gold generation per turn (listed next to the pile of gold), their current upgrade level (listed next to the arrow icon), the race inhabiting the town, and the race's relationship with you. If you own the town, you may enter the town's production screen by clicking on the enter icon as per other structures. Instead of clicking on the party floater to enter the town, you may also double-click on the town from the Main Map to bring up the town's screen.

Inside of a Town

After clicking on the Enter button from the Structure floater, the Town Screen appears. Town interface is not handled in a floater and functions separately from the Main Map. To close the Town Screen, hit the Exit button in the bottom right.

Population Information – The top-left box displays the current race inhabiting the town. The name of the race, its picture, its friendly terrain bonus, and the morale of the inhabitants are displayed in the top half of this box. In the bottom half, your race relations with the population and the strength of the occupational forces are listed.

Income Information – The middle box contains the economic breakdown of the town. The daily income, gained from the town size and crop fields, are listed. Any income-enhancing modifiers are listed in the income breakdown.

Enhancements – The top-right box displays any enchantments currently affecting the town. Enhancements listed here include the upgrade level, any wall type, and any spells affecting the town.

Production Information – Across the bottom of the town screen are the production information fields. The left-box list displays the current production queue the town is executing. The item ranked in the #1 slot will be built first and work will progress down the list. The Queue Repeat button to the right of the production list allows you to repeatedly build the same unit without constantly updating the production queue. To the right of the repeat button lies the production progression meter. All current projects have their name, and the turns remaining to completion, displayed here.

Changing the Production Queue

If you wish to modify the production queue, hit the Change button near the bottom right to bring up the production screen.

Production Screen

The Production Screen is where all types of upgrading, fortifying, and unit construction are handled. Units are displayed just beneath the town picture, and town projects are displayed near the bottom. To see a unit or project's information, click on it and the center fields will display all the available information. You may exit this screen at any time, by hitting the Done button near the bottom-right.

Units

Units are what your armies are made of, and towns are the quickest source of them. Units must be installed in order to be produced. To build an installed unit, select one from the list beneath the picture. You must have enough stockpiled gold to immediately pay the entire construction cost of the unit. If your gold is sufficient, you may immediately start building the selected unit by clicking the Produce button. If you wish to add more than one item to the production queue, hit the Queue button instead of Produce.

Installing New Units – All towns are capable of building four tier-one units, but no other units are guaranteed to be installed in a town. Currently un-installed, but installable units, appear dimmer next to already installed units. If there are no new units to install, you must first Upgrade the town, if the town's size permits it. When a unit is available for installation, select it from the list and hit the Install button to install it.

Projects

There are six types of non-unit productions that a city may undertake.

Produce Merchandise – Producing Merchandise increases the town's daily gold income by 25%. Select the project and hit the Produce Merchandise button to start the process. Producing merchandise is the default and idle state for all towns, so your towns will always be producing income.

Upgrade – Upgrading a town consumes two turns and requires 250 gold. A town can only be upgraded until its upgrade level equals its size. Upgrading typically adds new units for installation, improves your race relation with the population, and increases a town's base income.

Fortify – Fortifying is the process of building walls around your town. If a town has no walls, Fortifying it once builds wooden walls. If a town already has wooden walls, Fortifying it a second time improves the walls to stone walls. Fortifying always takes two turns and can be done twice, but larger size towns cost more money to fortify than smaller towns. Fortifying a town also improves your race relations with the population.

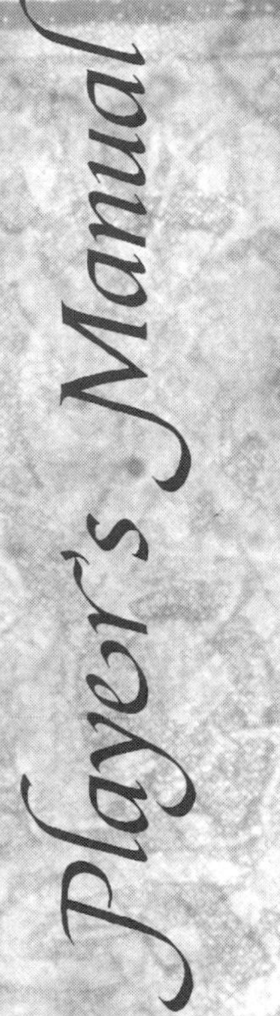

Migrate – Migrating replaces the current town's entire population with a new migrating race. When you select the Migrate project, the current population and your race relationship with them will be shown in the left box. The races available to replace the former population will be shown in the center box. Some races, depending on how far away they are from the city, will take longer to migrate. Replacing a population has a negative impact on your race relation with the old population, but a positive impact on your race relation with the new population. Select the race you wish to migrate to the town and hit the Migrate button to begin.

Loot – Looting is the process of stealing and plundering anything of value from a town and leaving it to die. Looting is a quick way to generate extra income, but the town will be destroyed after the looting process is complete, and your race relation with the former population will suffer. To loot a town, select the Loot project and hit the Loot button.

Raze – Razing burns the entire town to the ground. No money is generated from this project, and the town is immediately reduced to ruins. Razing a town severely penalizes your race relations with the town's former inhabitants. Select the Raze project and hit the Raze! button to turn the town to ashes.

Section Seven

Combat

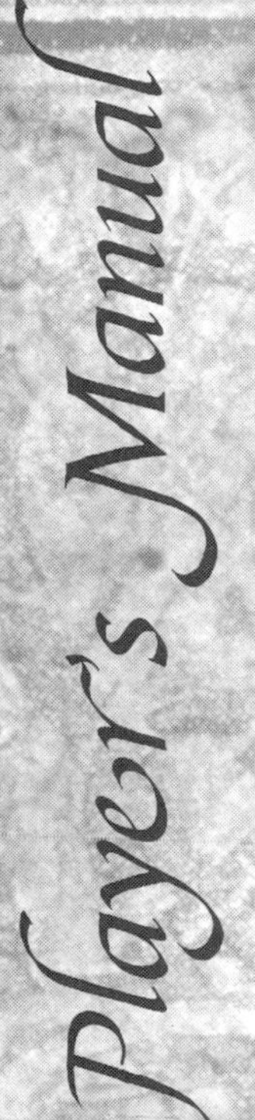

Combat

Though diplomacy is a powerful tool for the Leader of any nation, sometimes nothing will substitute for brute force. In the world of *Age of Wonders* your troops will be able to defeat enemy armies, annex towns and cities into your kingdom, explore ancient ruins, and perform other activities through the powerful combat interface.

A battle occurs whenever a stack of your units encounters enemy units, roving monsters, bandits, or other unfriendly forces on the global map. This can occur almost anywhere; in an open field on the map, inside a town or city, on the ocean, even inside ancient ruins. Your success in battle will rely on your knowledge of the different types of battle situations, and your application of the most effective tactics to each. What works well for an open field battle may not be the best strategy for the invasion of a city, and vice versa.

The Adjacent Hex Rule:

A note worth including here regards the Adjacent Hex Rule. To encourage tactics as well as brute strength, *Age of Wonders* will allow you to split your armies into multiple groups to attack an enemy from different paths during a battle. In order to take advantage of this, split your troops into up to six groups on the Global Map. When you surround a group of enemy units and attack them, with each of your groups adjacent to the enemy, all of your groups will join in the battle, and use more troops than you normally would have. The maximum number of troops in a stack is eight, but by taking advantage of the Adjacent Hex Rule, you can expand your army to a maximum of 48 troops during one battle (though the majority of battles will take place on a smaller scale). Due to the size and shape of the battlefield, your troop stacks to the immediate left and right of the enemy will not participate in the fight, so position your troops wisely. You must also consider this rule when defending your cities or other resources, as your opponent will also take advantage of the Adjacent Hex Rule when planning battles.

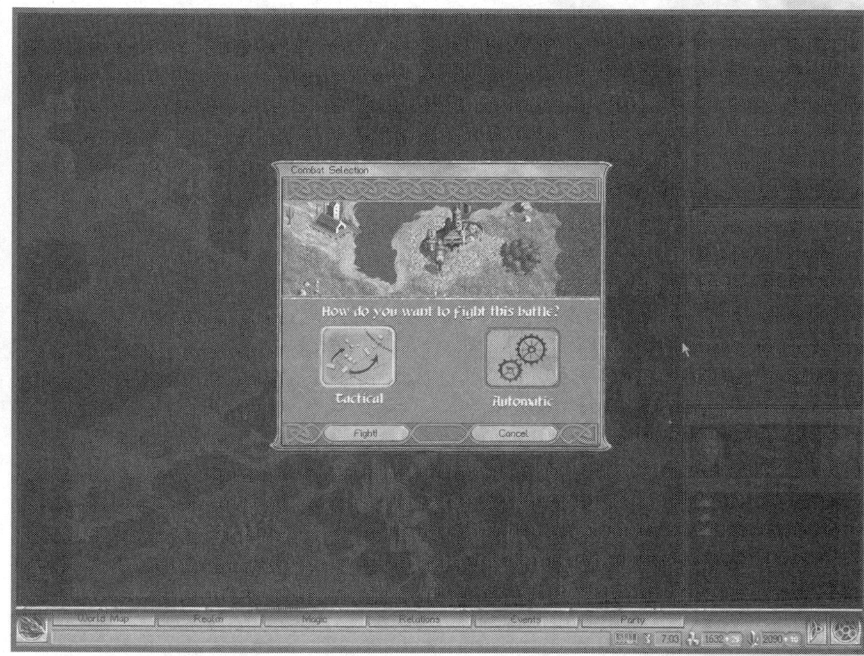

When a battle begins, a window will pop up asking whether you wish to have the battle resolved Automatically (with the computer controlling both sides) or in Tactical mode, where you will take command of your troops and fight the battle yourself. Automatic mode is much quicker than Tactical, but you face a greater risk of losing units during the battle.

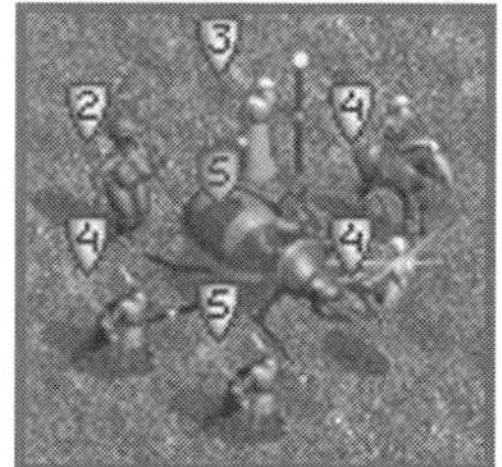

Using the adjacent hex rule, if any of these stacks of Elven units were to attack the Goblin Big Beetle in the middle, all of the other Elven stacks will automatically join in the battle.

Automatic Mode

If you chose to fight the battle Automatically, a screen will pop up that will begin to play out the battle in accelerated time, with the computer controlling both sides. You can slow down the battle or pause it if you wish, but you will have no direct control over your units. As the computer simulates the battle, you will be able to see the actions that your units take, and the damage they receive. Once all of the units on one side have been killed or otherwise incapacitated, the battle ends with the victorious side remaining on the world map.

Tactical Mode

If you choose to fight the battle in Tactical mode, you will be brought to a special Battle Map. This map will accurately reflect the terrain of the global map where the fight began. Towns will be recreated in detail, trees and stones will dot the landscape, and any structures nearby will show up on the map. All of these must be taken into account when planning movement or attacks.

Tactical battles are turn-based, with each unit able to perform one action, or use a certain number of movement points during that turn. After a unit has performed its actions for that turn, it will be immobile until the beginning of the next turn.

You begin a Tactical battle by looking at your troops, positioned on the Battle Map. Your units will appear with small red bars and spheres above them. The red bars are a health indicator, so you must monitor them carefully to tell which units are seriously injured. The spheres indicate which units are still capable of movement or action, and you can tell by the color what the affiliation of the unit is in multi-sided battles. As they perform actions through the battle, the spheres will blink if the unit still has movement or action allocated to it, and will stop blinking when the unit cannot move or do anything for the rest of the turn.

There are many different actions your units will be able to perform, but most of them fall under three categories:

Movement:

Movement is more or less self-explanatory. When you have a unit selected, you can click on a space in the map and that unit will try to find the best path to that space (as shown by a path of arrows). Click again and the unit will move to that space, or, if you change your mind, right click and the movement path will disappear. As on the Global Map, if the unit is unable to make the movement in one turn, the range of his movement will be represented by yellow arrows, with the area that he can't reach shown as gray arrows. Unlike the Global Map, however, your units will not be able to move to a space and perform any other action in the same turn. So, for instance, you cannot move your archer so an enemy soldier is just inside his range, and then fire; the enemy soldier would have to be inside his range at the beginning of the turn. The exception to this rule is any action that incorporates movement as part of the action itself (as do most melee attacks, see below).

Melee Actions:

Melee actions incorporate a wide variety of both offensive and defensive capabilities for your units, such as melee attacks, healing, crushing walls, and other useful actions. Melee attacks are the most common of these actions. If you wish to order a unit to attack, simply select that unit by clicking on it and drag your cursor over an enemy unit. The cursor should turn into a pair of swords, the attack cursor. Click on the enemy unit, and a path of arrows, similar to the ones shown when moving, will appear. If all the arrows are yellow, then the unit is able to reach the enemy and will be able to attack. If any of them are grey, then your unit will be unable to cover the distance to the enemy in a single turn. If you wish to continue with the attack, click again on the enemy unit, if not, right click anywhere on the screen and the attack will be canceled.

In the event that you continue with the attack, you must be careful. The enemy is not completely inanimate during your turn, and will attack your units as they pass close by, and counterattack when you attack them. If your attacker (or even a unit that is just moving) moves to or from a space directly next to an enemy unit, and if the enemy unit is capable of melee attacks, then the enemy unit will automatically get a free attack against your unit. This is the reason your units sometimes pick winding paths around the map to get to their destination. If you wish to move past an enemy unit, you can manually choose the path by clicking one square at a time along the path you wish to take.

You must also consider the counterattack. When your unit makes a melee attack against an enemy unit that can also make melee attacks, they will respond to your attacks by attacking you in turn. Once your unit reaches its target, it will perform its first swing (most melee units swing their weapons multiple times during an attack). If the enemy survives this swing, it will automatically swing back. Your unit attacks again, and your unit and the enemy exchange swings until the attack is complete (or one of the units dies).

Of course, there are many more types of Melee actions than just attacks. These will be listed in the unit's skill list (which appears in the right side of the screen when a unit is selected). In order to use these skills, select the unit, click on the skill you wish to use, and then click on the target in the main screen. The arrows along the ground will appear, letting you know if you can reach your target this turn. If you can cover the distance, click again, and the unit will automatically move to the target and use the skill you selected.

Ranged Actions:

Many units are capable of attacking from a distance in *Age of Wonders*. Archers, catapults, spell-casting Heroes, and other ranged units will give your armies greater flexibility than using melee units alone.

In order to use the Unit's Ranged attack, you must first select the unit by clicking on it. When it's active, its ability list will be displayed in the right side of the screen, with the actions you can select shown in white. Select the Ranged action you wish to use (e.g. Archery) and a red outline will appear on the Battle Map around the unit. This is the maximum range for the Ranged action you're attempting; your target must be within (or on) this red line or you will not be able to hit it. Assuming there is a valid target within the red outline, you can click on it to bring up a target line. This will outline the path the projectile (or spell) will take on the way to its target, shown as a dotted line.

If there is anything blocking the path to the target, a small circle will appear on the target line, with a number inside. This number is the chance that the projectile will hit the obstacle and be prevented from reaching the target, on a scale of 1-100, with 100 meaning the projectile has no chance of reaching its target. In cases where you can't find a clean shot at a target, you may wish to choose another target, or move the attacker to find a better angle of attack. Note that some Ranged attacks (such as the Halfling Slinger or the Ice Shards spell) will fire multiple projectiles with the same action. In this case, the chance that the shot will be blocked is calculated for each individual projectile, so even if the first projectile is blocked, some of the rest may make it to the target.

Types of Battles:

There are a few different types of battles that should be discussed before you begin your quest to conquer the Valley. While all battles are fought using the same interface, there are some tactical differences between the kinds of battles you'll be fighting.

Open-Field Battle

An Open-Field Battle is one that takes place away from a town in the open field of the Global Map. Since there are very few buildings to worry about, success in these types of battles generally depend on your skill at troop formations and positioning. You can take advantage of the Adjacent Hex Rule when planning to attack an enemy in the open field, and you should use it wisely, especially if the enemy is stronger than you are.

Town Battle

The focal points of the Global map in *Age of Wonders* are the Towns. Controlling the Towns that litter the landscape is crucial to sustained resource and unit production. Accordingly, you will occasionally find yourself wanting a town your opponent controls. When this happens, you'll have to send in your troops and try to take control of the town by force.

Battles in Towns take the same form as Open-Field battles, with a notable exception: Fortifications. When you control a Town, you will notice the option to build either Wood or Stone walls around the town to protect it from invaders. The computer has the same option, and will often fortify its towns as well. These are impassable to most units, and must either be destroyed or bypassed in order to engage your enemy in combat. If you attack a town, the enemy will be able to pass through the wall's gates during their turn, but the gates will automatically close during your turn, leaving you unable to enter the city. If you are fighting against the computer, it will know it has the advantage in this situation and will wait in the city until you are able to attack it.

Your troops here are prepared to break down the walls using their Catapults in order to engage the enemy, which hides behind the walls to avoid archer fire.

Having broken down the wall, your troops are prepared to enter the city and vanquish the remaining enemies.

You, as the attacker, have a few choices when dealing with the walls. You can attempt to break the walls down, using a unit with the Wall Crushing skill, or a unit that can hurl boulders or otherwise harm walls (such as Catapults). Once a section of wall is broken, your units will be able to pass through into the city and engage the garrison inside.

Battles in Ruins/Dungeons

Battles in ruins or dungeons can reap great rewards, but they are risky. The Adjacent Hex rule has no effect in these battles; you are only allowed one stack of eight units when you explore one of these locations. You also will not know what enemies you will face when you begin the fight, and the battleground will be covered when you begin the battle (if you choose to fight in Tactical mode), so you will not be able to see much of the area. That said, once all the enemies in one of these places are killed, you will be rewarded with either treasure, in the form of magical items that will enhance your Heroes, or freed prisoners who will join your cause.

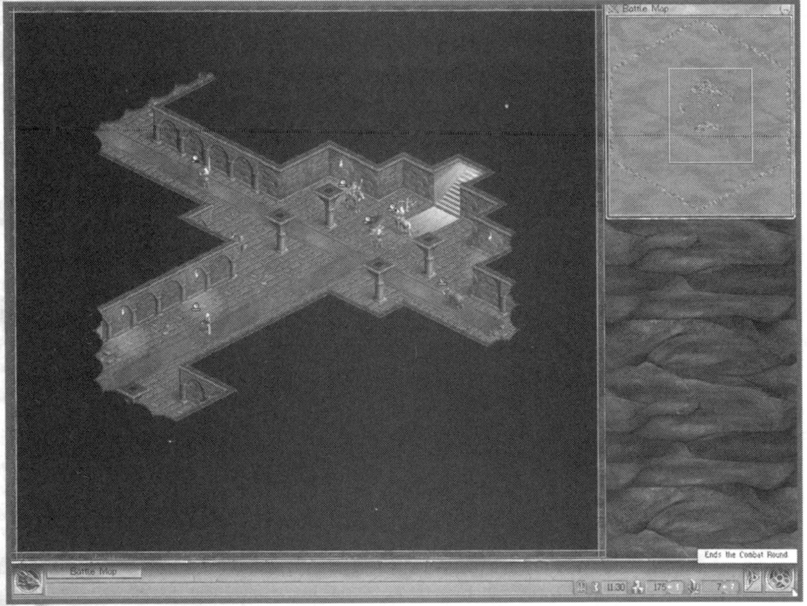

As this shows, you will not be able to see much of the area you're fighting in when you begin a battle in a ruin or dungeon.

Section Eight

Diplomacy

A Child of Hope

Elwyn's child Julia grew. She learned to foster the hope of peace, and many of the people in the land looked to her as the hope of a true heir to Inioch's fallen Kingdom. Inwardly they prayed that she might be the key to return the world to balance and stop the endless wars. She grew quickly among the Keepers, every day more eager to learn. They taught her the tokens and signs that controlled the very powers of Life.

Yet, despite her training, for two centuries the lands bathed in blood. Julia grew in the harsh realm of adversity, and came to know the workings of war, diplomacy, magic and power, but at the same time she learned to cherish the times of tranquillity, celebration, and joy that flitted about her in the form of dear friends. She knew the power of love and the dangers of hatred, and so it was that she learned wisdom.

Wars without Number

Every race allied with other races, and every race betrayed other races. At the center, the Human forces swelled and ebbed, yet always managed to hold the Valley of Wonders. Other factions gathered at the edges of the Chaos, hoping to steal the riches of Inioch's Kingdom, only to find the Humans an indomitable foe. The dead rose from the graves and strangled life. The earth was blackened with conflict. Famine and pestilence withered the many factions, but the fighting continued.

Then one day there was no battle. The next day no battle came, and the next. For ten years, war ceased, and the races built their arms, rebuilt their tattered cities and strengthened their holdings, expecting the other to attack, and still nothing came. They forged alliances, and plotted their subtle schemes, but for a decade all in the land poised ready, in silence, waiting for a sign to strike.

Signs and Wonders

The sign came in the form of a brilliant star, shining high in the sky directly over the ruins of Inioch's Court. From every point in the Kingdom, the star could be seen. Seers and Sages muttered cryptic warnings that the end was near, and that the world would never be the same. Within days of its appearance, Keeper spies spotted Meandor walking among the shadows of Inioch's ruined Court, searching for something.

As leader of the Keepers, Julia gathered her closest advisors and set off for the Valley of Wonders to rebut whatever conspiracy her half-brother had in mind. Unsuspectingly, she had already fallen for the first part of Meandor's plan to cripple the Keepers forever and obliterate the menacing race known as "Humans."

Race Relations and Diplomacy

Racial relations reflect the feelings between races; the diplomatic status describes the relation between players. Race relations have a fixed initial status, reflecting one race's prejudices towards another, based on the race's alignment. But all is subject to change. Diplomacy and race relations have a mutual impact on each other. Race relations will determine the likelihood of two players engaging in peace, war, or an alliance. On the other hand, diplomatic actions will greatly impact race relations. Breaking an alliance or peace treaty will not only affect the relation with the race in question, but also on other races, including your own, depending on their individual relations towards you. Elves get along pretty well with Halflings and will not appreciate your breaking an alliance with a traditional ally. Diplomatic actions have a chain reaction effect.

Diplomacy and race relations form a dynamic whole, and both influence all aspects of your empire, from the morale of units and cities, to the chance of independents joining. You should carefully consider the tradeoffs of diplomatic, tactical, and strategic actions.

The Relations Interface

The Relations menu is accessed from the Relations button in the bottom menu bar.

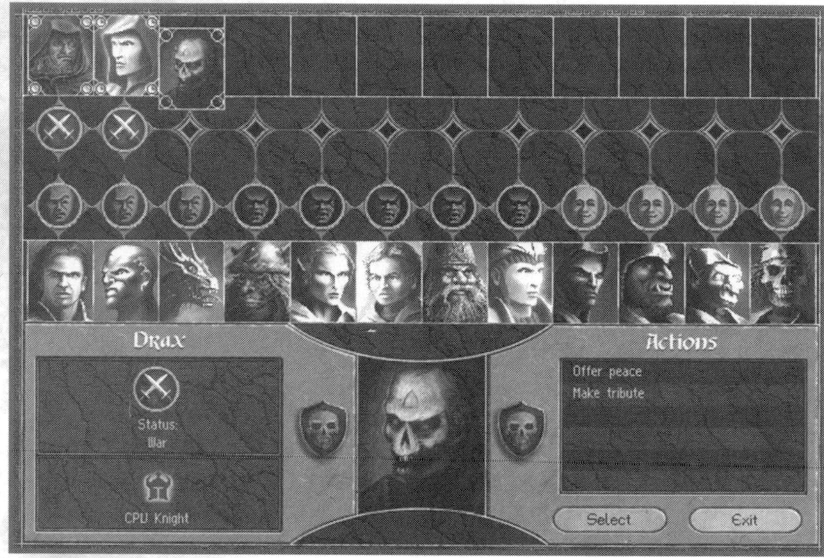

Understanding the Relations Menu

A list of all the Leaders you have met is displayed across the top left. Your picture will always be shown, but you must make contact with a separate player's forces before their Leader's picture will be displayed.

Diplomatic Statuses

For the players to engage in diplomatic action, their forces will need to meet on the Main Map. The diplomatic status changes from No Contact to Unknown, and diplomatic actions can be undertaken.The bottom left field displays your diplomatic status with a selected Leader and what type of AI or human controls the Leader. The following diplomatic statuses are possible.

No Contact – Starting condition to all players who haven't met in the scenario.

Unknown – Players have met, but no diplomatic action has taken place.

War – Players are engaged in open hostile actions.

Peace – Players have agreed not to attack each other. Players who will suffer heavy losses are more likely to accept peace, so they will have a chance to rebuild.

Alliance – Players work together in fighting common enemies. Allied players have access to each other's visibility range. Allies fight together in battles using the adjacent hexagon rule. If the Allied Victory option is enabled, allies are capable of jointly winning a scenario.

Diplomatic Actions

When a Leader is selected from the top row, the bottom right field displays any available diplomatic actions you may present to the selected Leader. To try a diplomatic action, highlight one from the list and click on the Select button.

Declare War – Formally declares a war against another race. This action is available from the No Contact, Peace, and Alliance statuses.

Offer Peace – Attempts to end hostilities or the possibility of hostilities between players. Available from the No Contact and War statuses. The recipient must accept the offer for it to take affect. You may include a tribute to the other player to increase your chances of him accepting your offer.

Propose Alliance – Offers a formal Alliance to the player. You may only offer alliances to players with whom you are at peace. Like a peace offering, the other player must accept the offer for the alliance to be formed, and you may offer a tribute to him when sending the proposal.

Break Alliance – Terminates an alliance with another player. Only available after already establishing an alliance with the player.

Threaten to Attack – When you are at peace or in an alliance with another race, you may threaten to attack them in an attempt to earn support or money. Threatening a race you are already at war with has no effect.

Make Tribute – Offers an amount of gold and/or mana to the player. The other player may refuse the offer if they like. Tributes often precede other diplomatic actions, like peace offers.

Send Message – For multiplayer games only, allows you to convey a text message to another player.

End Alliance with Other Player – Asks the player if they are willing to end their alliance with a third player with whom they have an alliance. You may suggest this as long as you have a peace or alliance with the player.

Declare War on Other Player – Asks the player to declare open hostilities against a third player. Only available when you have a standing peace or alliance with the player.

Gold and mana used for tributes is subtracted as soon as the diplomatic action is sent, but if the offer is declined or not answered within one turn, the gold is returned.

Race Relations

A key element of Age of Wonders is the race relation model. It describes the status between the races and determines the interaction with other sides or independents. Every race has a unique status towards other races, be it independents or sides. These relations have an initial status that changes during the course of play.

Selecting a race displays a face icon above or below each Leader and race representing their relationship with the selected race.The race statuses are displayed in various places in the game, with the main representation being the Relations screen. Race Relation statuses are often displayed by faces exhibiting different features. Relations are: Friendly, Polite, Neutral, Wary and Hate. Friendly face icons represent positive relations, while hostile face icons represent a negative race relation.

Each race has their portrait displayed across the bottom row. Selecting a race will cause the lower left field to display their racial information.

Section Nine

Fighting Units

Units

Units are the mainstays of any combat force in *Age of Wonders*. While it is true that Heroes can be some of your most powerful allies, most of your forces will undoubtedly be Units.

Units come in MANY varieties in *Age of Wonders*. A Unit can fill the role of anything from ranged attacker to close combat melee unit. It is usually a good idea to mix the units in a party by including cavalry, melee, ranged, as well as flying units.

All of your Units have certain statistics and special abilities that will affect their actions on both the Global and Battle maps. You can view these at any time by clicking the unit in either the Global or Battle maps; a small text window should appear with the basic information about the unit. When you are choosing which unit to build or summon, keep in mind that higher Statistics are better. There are six statistics that are core to both Units and Heroes, in that they act pretty much the same for both. Beyond the six core statistics, Units have several other statistics, some that are similar to those of Heroes, and some that are completely their own. For your convenience, there is a list of every unit of the twelve racial affiliations in Appendix 1.

The six core statistics

Attack

This is the chance that a unit's attack will damage an enemy unit. When you attempt an attack, the computer will calculate a chance for a hit based on your unit's Attack number and the enemy unit's Defense number. If the attack is unsuccessful, nothing happens. If the attack is successful, though, you move to the calculation of Damage from the attack.

A higher number here is better, but the game calculates the success of the attack based on the difference between the attacker's Attack number and the enemy's Defense number, so you should also check your target's Statistics before attacking, to make sure their Defense isn't too high above your Attack stat (or your chances of hitting them will be very poor).

Ranged Attacks, such as Archery or ranged spells, have their own Attack numbers, so you don't have to worry about your Archer's low Attack. When you select a Ranged Attack, a small window will appear below the miniature Combat map in the upper right corner of the screen. This will show the Ranged Attack's Attack and Damage statistic, as well as what type of damage it does and any other special information.

Damage

A Unit's Damage number helps determine how much damage the unit will deal to an enemy when it successfully completes an attack. When a unit hits an enemy, the computer will calculate the damage dealt from the Damage number and the difference between the attacker's Attack and the enemy's Defense. So, even if your low-Attack Unit manages to hit the enemy's high-Defense Unit, it won't do as much damage as it would against a Unit with less Defense. Keep this in mind when choosing who to attack.

As with the Attack stat, Ranged Attacks will have their own separate Damage number.

Defense

As mentioned above, the Defense number has an effect on both the chances an enemy will be successful in hitting your unit, and the amount of damage the enemy will deal if it successfully completes the attack. In general, Units with higher Defense numbers will have a better chance of surviving an attack than Units with lower Defenses.

Health

Health determines the amount of damage a unit can sustain before it dies and can no longer be used. Of course, a higher number will let a Unit take more damage and engage in more combat before it dies. Some Units, such as Clerics, and some spells, such as Remedy, can heal Units, restoring lost hit points in the middle of battle. Outside of battle, all Units will regain lost hit points slowly over a few turns. You can also station your troops in a town to allow them to heal more quickly.

Movement

A Unit's Movement points will affect how far it can move on both the Global Map and the Combat map. Typically, 4 movement points will be deducted for every space the Unit moves on the Global Map across an open plain, but that can be affected by the terrain. Roads and Enchanted roads will allow your units to travel farther with the same amount of Movement points. Forests will slow down Units, unless they have the Forestry ability, which allows them to travel normally through forests. If a Unit has the Mountaineering ability, it will be able to walk across Mountains, but if it does not, the unit will be prevented from passing Mountains at all, and will have to find a way around them. The same situation is presented with Oceans: if a unit has the Swimming ability, it will be able to cross over Oceans and rivers, but units without the ability will have to find a way around (or get a ship to take them across).

Some units are able to Fly. Units with this ability will be able to cross all types of terrain, but tall mountains may slow them down somewhat.

When several types of Units are grouped together in a party, the lowest common denominator determines the movement for the whole party. For instance, suppose you are playing the Halflings, and your Leader has been trained with Mountaineering and Forestry, and has a movement of 33. He bands with a Halfling Swordsman who has a movement of 24, and an Eagle Rider who can Fly and has a movement of 40. The Party would be restricted to the movement of the Halfling Swordsman because the Halfling Swordsman's movement is the lowest common denominator. Since he only has a movement of 24, the rest of the party is restricted to 24. The Halfling Swordsman also does not have Flying, as with your Hero, so your party cannot fly, and since the Halfling Swordsman does not have Mountaineering, your party cannot cross mountains. If you needed to cross a Mountain, you would have to leave the Halfling Swordsman behind, but the others could cross, as the hero has the Mountaineering skill, and the Eagle Rider can fly. If you needed to cross a body of water, only the Eagle Rider would be able to do that.

Resistance

Resistance determines how well a Unit will be able to resist the effects of magic, poison, and other types of non-physical damage. Having a high Resistance also helps in combat.

Section Ten

Heroes

Heroes

Heroes can be some of the hardest hitters in *Age of Wonders*. While initially they may not be the strongest of units, they are not as limited as regular units are in how many levels they can achieve. A Hero might start anywhere between level 1 and level 6, and progress from there by gaining experience through various means. As Heroes gains experience, you may choose new abilities for them – anything from movement to combat enhancements.

At the beginning of a Campaign you typically start with your Leader, and occasionally a Hero as well. New Heroes come about in one of two ways. Sometimes a new Hero will appear upon the map; while this is highly random, it typically happens after you perform several deeds that have inspired a Hero to join your cause. Heroes can also appear on the map through the Summon Hero spell.

Your Leader is a Hero. This is important to remember because he will have the same advantages and disadvantages as any other Hero, and other races will react to your Leader the same way as they would to any other Hero of the same race. The main difference is that your Leader is you, in the game. If your Leader dies, your game is over.

When you click on your Hero, and then click on his picture in the right-hand side of the screen, a window with information about your Hero is displayed, as is shown below.

This screen shows your Hero, his statistical characteristics, abilities, level and experience, which are explained below, as well as a blue symbol that denotes mana production. The hero's Mana Production is calculated by adding 5 for the spell casting ability, and then by multiplying 5 times the spell casting *level* and adding it to the initial 5. The higher your spell casting, the more mana you will have. Clicking the Info tab in this window will bring up information on what spheres of magic your Hero has, as well as information pertaining to your racial relations with that Hero.

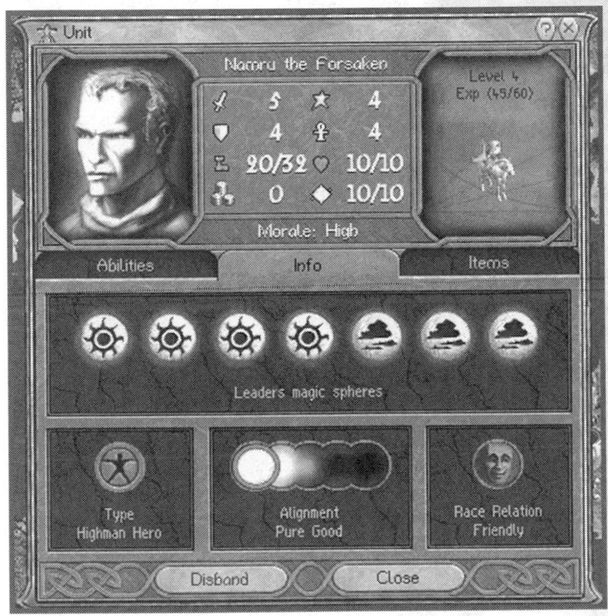

As discussed later in the Magic section (page 83), the spheres of magic that your Hero studies can drastically influence how he is played. The information pertaining to his racial ties can also influence his role in the game. For instance, if a Hero is of the same race as your Leader, and you have maintained good relations with your own race, the Hero will be inclined to join you. Also, if a Hero is of a race which you have declared war on, watch him closely as he might betray you.

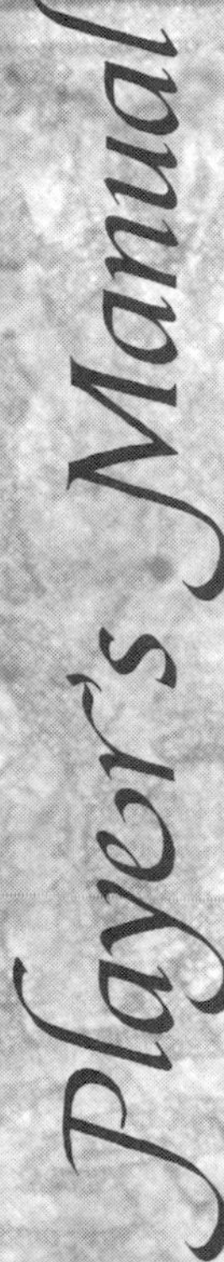

The third section of this window is Items. The Items window shows what Items your Hero has, and what Items, if any, are on the ground where your Hero is. Don't worry about trying to check every bit of ground for Items, because if they are on the ground, there will be a bag in the location where they are. Items and their uses are described in the Items section shown below.

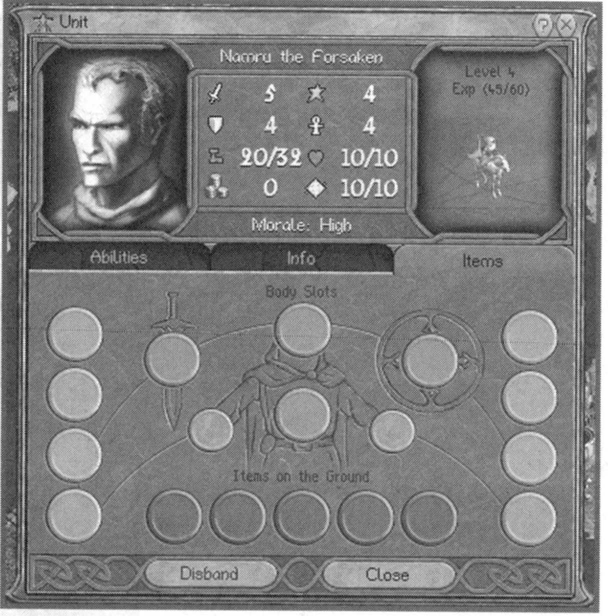

Each Hero has a name, title, the same six basic statistics that Units have (see Fighting Units, Page 73), and four extended statistics, along with several abilities (both selected and fixed). The four extended statistics are as follows.

Race

This is the Hero's race. A Hero can be any of the twelve races found in *Age of Wonders*. It is important that you check a hero's race and the relations that you have with that race, especially when you first encounter the Hero. Depending upon your relations with the race of any new Heroes you see, they might either attack you, or join you.

Experience

Experience is displayed by a fraction with the numerator representing the current experience that the Hero has gained, and the denominator representing the amount of experience that the Hero needs to achieve the next level. Heroes go up in level rather slowly. They can gain Experience by fighting in combat, or by just letting turns go by. Experience is critical to a strong Hero.

Level

The level of a Hero is an indirect indicator of the power of a Hero. The higher the Hero's level, the more skill points that Hero gets to spend on abilities. In this manner, Heroes can increase their leadership, sight distance, marksmanship, or any number of other abilities. A Hero can attain a peak level of 30.

Gender

Heroes, like units, have a Gender. While Units have 3 possible Genders (male, female, and neuter), Heroes tend to come as Males or Females.

Items

Items are used by Heroes to both enhance their usefulness on the global map, as well as on combat maps. A given Item can have an effect upon the Hero, ranging anywhere from giving new abilities, to granting a better defense or stronger attack. Gathering Items for your Hero is vital to his success, and to increasing their strength.

You can find Items in several places on the Global Map. They tend to be found in Ruins or Ziggurats, and sometimes Monster Dens; however, they can also be found after killing a Hero that had one or two.

Items come in 6 varieties: Attack, Defense, Torso, Head, Ring, and Use. It is ideal to have at least one of each in their proper position.

Attack

Attack items are things like Swords or Battle Axes. Typically they enhance either Attack or Damage, and sometimes both. They also tend to add to a Hero's abilities, by adding abilities like Strike or Magic Strike. All Heroes have the melee strike ability.

Defense

Defense items are shields. They tend to enhance a Hero's Defense; however, they can also enhance Resistance and grant the Hero special abilities that help in protecting the Hero, like Fire Resistance or Cold Resistance.

Torso

Torso items come in two varieties: body armor and cloaks. They tend to enhance Defense and/or Resistance; however, they can also add abilities. Typically the abilities that come from Torso items are better than those from Defense items, dealing bonus abilities such as Fire Immunity or Cold Immunity.

Head

Head items are items worn on the head, like Crowns or Helms. They tend to bestow abilities that either increase the sight abilities of your Hero, or help in their defense, like True Seeing or Death Protection.

Ring

Ring items are items that tend to grant either statistical increases or abilities. The name of the ring tends to signify which abilities it bestows. Rings generally do not grant statistical increases and abilities at the same time.

Use

Use items are items that convey no statistical increases or new abilities. They are used during combat to grant special forms of attack that the Hero would not otherwise have.

Section Eleven

Magic

Magic

Magic is a powerful force in *Age of Wonders*. Using your Leader and spell-casting Heroes, you will be able to use magic to dramatically change the landscape of the map, summon fantastic creatures to fight alongside you, hurl damaging spells at enemy units, and more.

There are seven different spheres of magic in *Age of Wonders*, each with its own unique spells and attributes. Below is a list of each sphere along with some basic spells.

Life: Born of the powers of creation and light, the sphere of Life endows its adherents with the power to heal and protect the living, as well as oppose the forces of evil and death.

Death: Many worshippers of the sphere of Death are twisted and evil creatures, more dead than alive. Most spells in this sphere deal with the destruction of life or involve attempts to escape the natural cycle of life by becoming undead.

Earth: The sphere of earth is subtle, yet powerful. While it isn't as effective at direct damage as its counterparts, it makes up for this by giving its worshippers the ability to move quickly, mine resources more efficiently, and even reshape the very ground around them.

Air: The most ethereal of the spheres, Air worshippers can control the weather and climate almost at will. This allows them to speed their movement or call great thunderstorms to strike down their enemies.

Fire: A dramatic, forceful sphere that represents the chaos of nature. While not seen as purely destructive, being a force of change and evolution, the Fire sphere is the sphere best suited to combat due to its offensive capabilities.

Water: The Water sphere is closely tied to Life, water being a necessity for all living things. In addition, disciples of Water gain control over bodies of water and vapor.

There are also two kinds of magic that can be learned by any Leader, of any sphere.

Cosmos: The Cosmos sphere contains general spells that are available to all magic users, regardless of which spheres they worship.

Special: The Special sphere of spells contains powerful magic that cannot be learned, but must be discovered through your adventures.

No matter which side you play, your Leader will determine the spheres of magic your side can worship. You can choose to dedicate more picks to a specific sphere, if you want to access the most powerful magic, or you can spread your picks among the spheres, to gain more versatility. The level of spells you can research in a sphere is dependent on the number of picks you dedicate to that sphere's worship. For example, if you have 3 picks of the Water Sphere, you will be able to cast level 1, 2, and 3 Water spells. However, each sphere opposes another sphere, and if you choose to worship a sphere, you cannot worship the opposing sphere.

Earth opposes Air

Fire opposes Water

Life opposes Death

The amount of sphere picks varies depending on the scenario. In general, the larger the scenario map, the more picks the Leader will have. In the single player campaign, the amount of spheres the Leader can access will increase as you progress through the game.

Spell Types

There are a few different magic types that you will use throughout the game. A basic knowledge of these types of magic is crucial to your success!

Global spells: Spells in the Global section of your spellbook can only be cast on the global map. There are a wide variety of Global spells, ranging from minor incantations that provide information about the kingdom, summon spells that bind magical creatures to your will, powerful attack magic that can devastate entire cities, and more. Global spells are split into three basic subdivisions.

Enchantment: Most (but not all) spells that have permanent effects and persist from turn to turn are enchantments. Enchantments require an infusion of mana every turn to maintain their potency. If you are unable to provide enough mana each turn to maintain your enchantments, your mana income will turn into a deficit, and you will lose mana each turn instead of gaining it. Once your mana reserves run out, your enchantments will begin to cancel themselves until your mana production is positive again. If your mana income turns negative, you may wish alter your magic balance away from Research and toward Mana (see "Magic Management" below). In any case, if you wish to cancel an Enchantment, you can do this through the Magic menu on the Global map. The enchantments that affect the entire map will appear under the "Global" tab, while the enchantments that affect only a small area (such as a town) will appear under the "Spell" tab.

These pictures were taken before and after Flood, a powerful Water spell, was cast. Global Enchantments such as these have the ability to radically change the flow of a game.

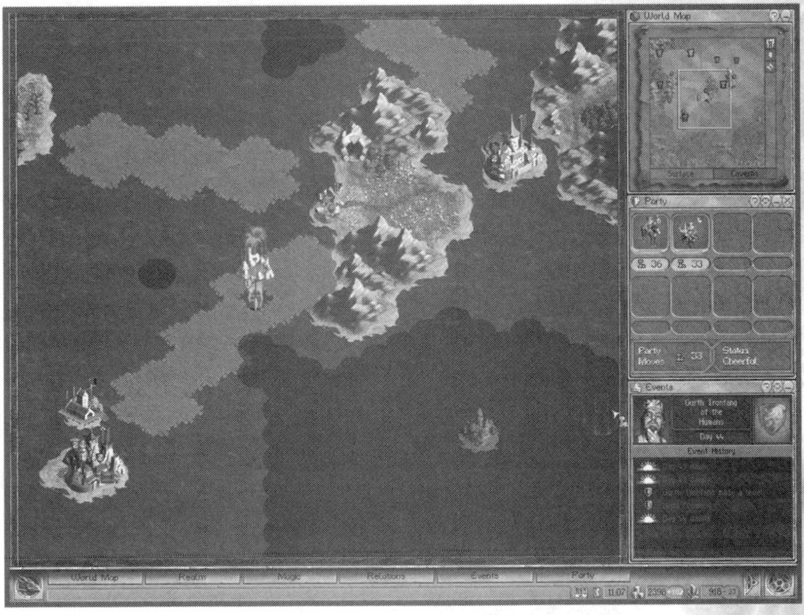

Summon: Summon spells bind the magic energy of certain exotic creatures to your will, allowing you to control them on the global map and in battle. Like Enchantments, once a Summon spell is cast, it will drain mana from you every turn until the creature dies, or you choose to cancel the spell (note that if you disband the creature, it will still drain mana from you). When a creature is summoned, it is placed in the same stack as the caster. If there isn't room in the caster's stack, a new stack will be created for the creature in an available adjacent space. You can cancel a Summon Spell by going to the "Spells" tab in the Magic menu, selecting the spell, and clicking on the "Remove" button.

Using Summon spells, you can summon armies such as these in a fraction of the time it would take to build the same amount of units. Mana costs can be prohibitive, though, as mana is generally found in lesser quantities than gold.

Instant: Instant spells cast on the Global map only have a casting fee, they do not drain mana every turn as Summon and Enchantment spells do. These generally have a short-term effect, such as Bird's Eye, which reveals a large area of the map when cast, but has no long-term effect on the game. Some, however, will permanently affect the game, such as Holy Woods, which grows a barrier of trees on the landscape that persists from turn to turn, but requires no sustained mana expenditure.

Using the Freeze Water spell, Gurth Ironfang has been able to cross previously impassable bodies of water quickly. This is an example of a Global Instant spell; though the water remains frozen, there is no sustained mana cost from turn to turn.

Unit Spells: Unit Spells are cast on your units, giving them temporary or permanent enhancements. Most unit spells deal enhanced combat prowess or affect movement, but others have more exotic effects. Unit spells can always be cast on the Global map, and most (but again, not all) can be cast during combat as well. These are divided into two different subdivisions.

Enchantments: As in the case of Global Enchantments, Unit Enchantments enhance your unit with a permanent enhancement at the cost of some mana every turn. These are generally less expensive than Global Enchantments, as they only affect one unit, as opposed to the entire battlefield. If you wish to cancel a Unit Enchantment, open the Magic menu and select the "Spells" tab; the spell and its target will be listed below. Select the spell and click "Remove" to cancel the spell.

Instant: Unit Instant spells are similar to Global Instant spells. These have an immediate effect that does not persist from turn to turn, but instead acts immediately for a one-time cost.

Combat Spells: Combat spells can only be cast during a battle. These are usually offensive spells that damage your enemies, but some Combat spells have less obvious effects, such as resurrecting dead units or slowing your enemy's movement across the battlefield. In order to cast these spells, you must have a Leader or Hero with the Spell-Casting ability in the battle.

The spell-caster here is trying to hit the Goblin Spearman with an Ice Shards spell during combat. Unfortunately, the Spearman has placed himself behind a wall that will block the spell. A wise Leader would cancel the spell here and choose another action. For more information on casting spells in combat, see the Ranged Action section, in the Combat chapter.

Casting Spells

To cast a spell, click on the Hero or Leader you wish to have cast the spell. In the Party window, click on the icon of the Hero. Another window will pop open, showing the Hero's abilities. Click on Spell Casting. Your Spell Book will appear. You can flip through the pages and select the spell you wish to cast, and cast it by clicking on it. Some spells may take more than one turn to cast, depending on how difficult they are and your caster's current Channeling skill. If you choose to cast it anyway, you will not be able to cast any other spells on the Global map until the first one is complete. In this case, you'll need to keep track of how many turns the spell will take to cast, and when it's complete, you can open your Hero's spell book again and cast another spell.

When a spell is cast, you will usually have to select a target for it on the Global map. Spells that affect everything in a small area will show the target cursor as well as a small red radius of effect, so you can choose where you want to cast the spell for maximum effect. Some spells will require an individual unit as a target; in that case, on the Global Map, click on the stack that the unit is in, and select it.

The process is similar in the case of casting spells during Combat. If you wish to cast a Combat spell, select the Hero or Leader you wish to cast the spell by left-clicking on him or her. The information window will pop up with the list of the Hero's abilities. Click on Spell-Casting, and the Spell Book will pop up. Select the Combat or Unit spell you wish to cast, a target (if required) and click again, and the spell will be cast immediately.

Magic Management

The "Magic" button on the row of buttons at the bottom of the screen will be your main interface for changing your magic settings. By clicking on the button, you will raise a small menu of magic options. There are 4 tabs on the menu:

Main: This shows your current power breakdown, and also what spell you are currently researching. You can click on the buttons beneath the two options to change your power structure, or select a new spell to research.

Spells: This tab shows the spells that are currently active and draining mana from you every turn, such as Summon spells and Unit enchantments. If you wish to regain the mana, or find the spell has lost its usefulness, you can highlight a spell and press the "Remove" button to cancel the spell.

Global: This tab shows the currently active Global enchantments and who owns them. You can also use the "Remove" button to cancel any Global enchantments of yours that are no longer useful.

Power: This shows all the current sources of your power, from Heroes, Nodes and your Leader.

Mana/Research

In order to use magic effectively, you will require both Mana and Research. Mana is somewhat similar to gold, except you use it to cast spells. Spells have different mana costs according to their power, and accordingly, higher-level spells generally become more expensive since they are more powerful. You will be provided a certain amount of Mana Crystals each turn, according to your Magic Power.

Your Research skill is needed to research new spells. You can research one spell at a time. Higher level spells generally take longer to research, compared to lower level spells. Increasing the Research allotment of your Magic Power will enable you to research spells more quickly, but your Mana Crystal income will be diminished.

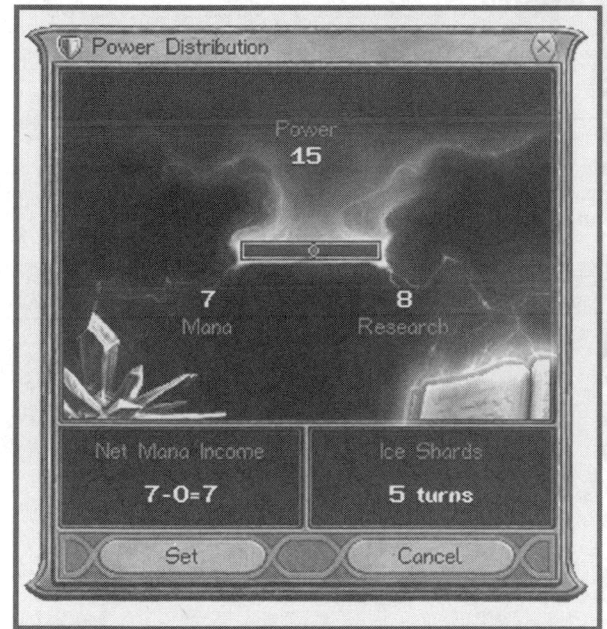

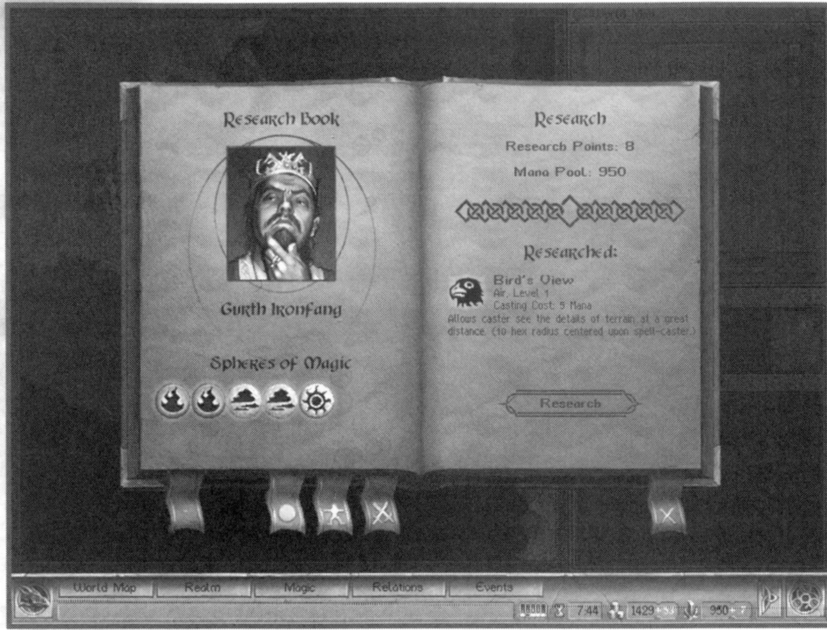

When you finish Researching a spell, this screen will appear, showing the spell you just researched and information about your Leader. Click on the "Research" button to begin research on another spell.

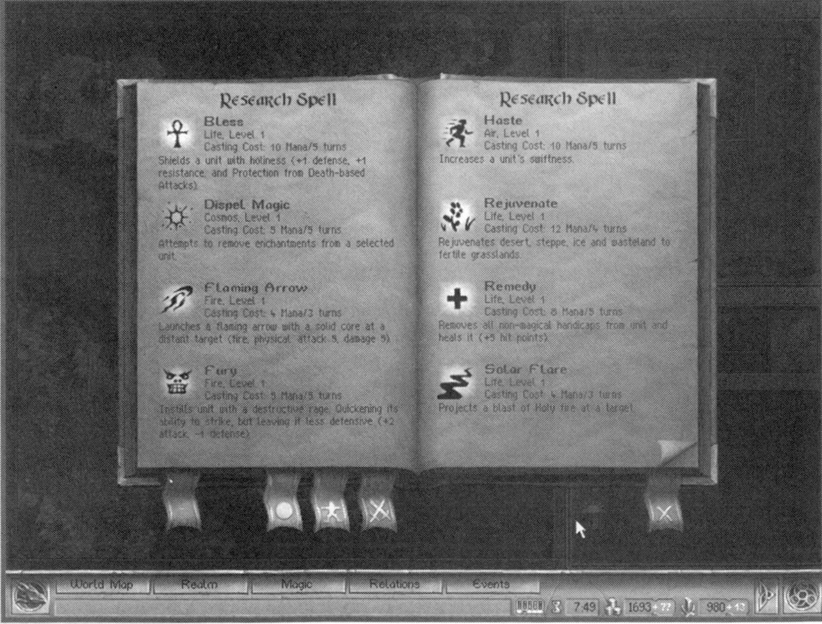

This is where you choose your next spell to research. Next to the Casting Cost is the number of turns it will take you to research the spell. Simply click on the spell you wish to obtain, and your Leader will begin research immediately.

Magic Power

Magic Power determines both your Research and Mana Crystal income.

Power is generated by spell-casting Heroes and all Leaders at the rate of 5 times the Hero's spell casting ability level (plus an additional 5 mana per turn in the case of the Leader). There are 5 successive levels of spell-casting ability that you can acquire as your characters gain levels.

Power Nodes generate mana. For every sphere of magic, excluding the Cosmic sphere, there is an ultimate mastery spell. One of the mastery spell's side affects is that when it is cast, a powerful creature aligned to the sphere of magic will appear at each power node belonging to the spell's sphere. (For example, fire mastery will summon fire elementals at all Fire Nodes). The creature is under the control of whoever owns the node.

Cosmic Nodes: These provide 10 power to their controller per turn, no matter what spheres he or she worships.

It's worth noting that your Mana Crystal income will be diminished if you cast a spell with a maintenance cost. Spells with maintenance costs require a certain amount of mana every turn to remain active. Keep this in mind when allocating your Magic Power.

Spell Casting Ability

Your Leader and Heroes with the Spell Casting ability will be able to wield magic to aid your cause. Your Leader and all of your Heroes that can cast spells will draw from the same spell book. Increasing this skill will bring you more Magic Power each turn, and it also determines how much mana the Leader/Hero can channel each turn.

Channeling (Points)

This determines the amount of Mana Crystals a Hero/Leader can use per turn. This counts both in and out of battle, so if you cast an expensive spell before a fight, you might be unable to cast combat spells. If your spell casting unit begins to cast a spell that has a cost greater than his available channeling allotment, the cost will be spread out over several turns until the casting is complete. Each spell casting unit can channel 10 times his or her Spell Casting ability level per turn.

Section Twelve

Races

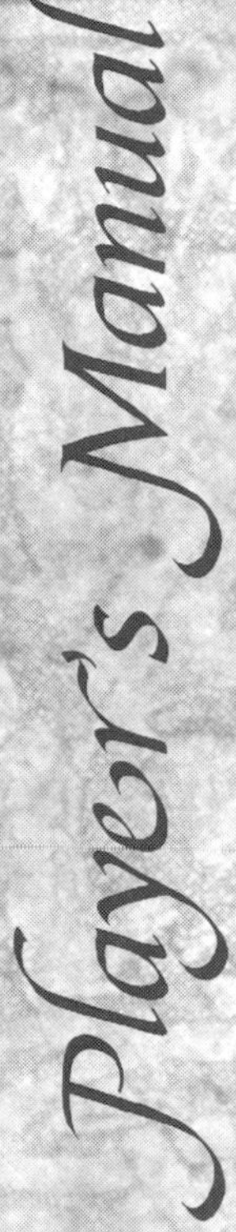

Races of the Valley of Wonders

The setting for *Age of Wonders* is highly influenced by the fantasy races dwelling in the game world. In any mode of play much revolves around making strategic use of the main race under your control, along with its allies, to overcome all foes on the map. With a total of 12 dominant races in the game, each with different backgrounds and tendencies, the possibility exists for an almost limitless amount of unique scenarios, strategies, and interactions. The following is a short description of each of the races in *Age of Wonders*.

Age of Wonders divides the 12 races into three categories: Good, Neutral, and Evil. The interaction between these three factions plays a very important role in which side you choose. For instance, initially you are on good terms with those races that are part of the same factions as you are, and can typically bribe them to join you, provided you have enough gold in your coffers.

You can also get races from opposing factions to join you by improving your diplomatic relations with them – by either migrating enough of your towns to their race, or by assisting them. Examples of assisting another race would include rejuvenating their farms or killing enough of their enemies. For instance, if you are playing the Humans, and you want to align yourself with the Dark Elves, killing enough Elves could prove very beneficial to your cause. While it is easy for a neutral race to align itself with either a good or evil race, it can be rather difficult for an evil race to align itself with a good race. This can make it much easier for the neutral player, as neutrals can always align themselves with the stronger faction.

The Elves

General: Elves are a thin, fragile-looking folk who typically dwell deep within the forest. Aside from their pointed ears and thin facial features, Elves look very similar to Humans. Although somewhat slimmer than Humans, their lean, muscular limbs give them great agility and speed. Elves can live forever and can only die by violence, but most choose, at a very old age to set sail for The Isle of Last Goodbyes in search of the mystical Isle of Evermor.

Society: Elves make their homes in forests where they feel at one with the natural beauty of their surroundings. Due to their immortality, unlike Dwarves and Humans, Elves are never in a rush and have little interest in short-term gains. Elves take pleasure in the finer points of life, including the arts and music, and most practice other skills unrelated to their chosen career paths. Elves value freedom and love above all. They recognize only a few lords, leaders who have proven themselves worthy of this title.

Combat: Elves are able to excel in many areas – hand-to-hand combat, archery, magic and stealth – making them a tough race to defeat. Slightly weaker in physical strength, Elven infantry and cavalry tend to rely on skill more than brute force. They are cautious warriors, swift but somewhat fragile, so they plan their attacks carefully. The support of their good allies and woodland creatures also adds to their formidability in times of war.

The Dwarves

General: Dwarves are small, stocky humanoids known for their industriousness and tenacity in battle. They usually live in elaborate underground cities, built beneath mountains, but can adapt to almost any climate. Dwarves harbor a deep respect for the earth and rock, stable things that stand the test of time.

Society: Almost all Dwarves are warriors, inventors, or hard laborers. Dwarves have a very strict work ethic, and do not believe in leisure or wasting time. They are also very family-oriented folk, and it is common for businesses and occupations to be handed down through many generations.

Although they will freely cooperate with the other good, and sometimes neutral, races, Dwarves tend to look down upon those who do not work as hard as they do and waste too much time on entertainment.

Combat: Dwarves make some of the fiercest warriors in all the lands. They prefer a good close-quarters fight to the use of magic and missile weapons, but that does not stop them from laying siege to well-fortified cities with archers and bombards. Although they look down upon stealth tactics, they have been known to attack from underground caves and over mountains to gain the element of surprise.

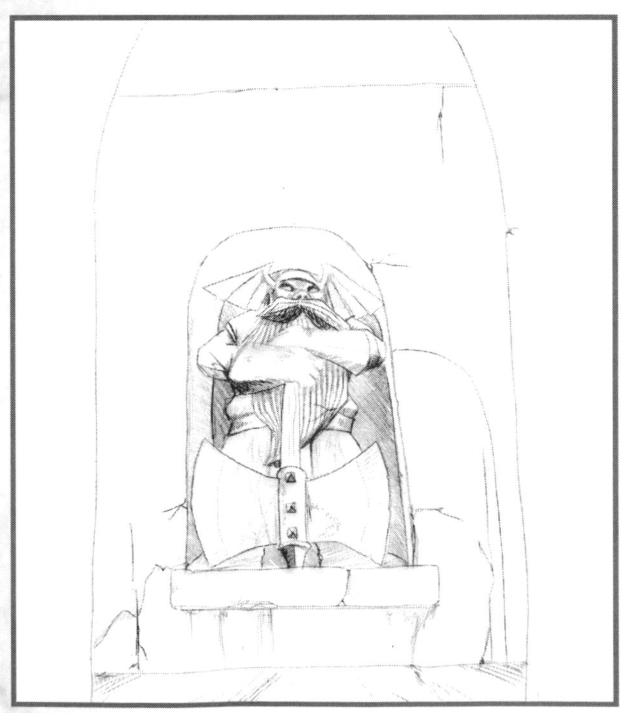

The Halflings

General: Halflings are a small, peaceful race of humanoids. Outgoing and cheerful, Halflings lead a pastoral life emphasizing comfort. Halflings are not likely to go on adventures, as such endeavors make one late for dinner.

Society: Halfling society is one of harmony and peace. Villages can be made up of as few as two or three families. They farm and trade with close neighbors like the Elves and Dwarves. Even in old age, Halflings manage to remain cheerful and productive. They work hard at their businesses, but work is rarely their primary focus.

Combat: Even though war can be brutal, Halflings tend not to take it seriously. They cope by telling tales and retreating to thoughts of more pleasant things, when not engaged in combat. Nevertheless, Halflings make fine warriors, as they are able to use their nimbleness and size to evade their opponents, taking the offensive when they see an opening in the enemy's defenses. Halflings are very resourceful in times of war, employing allies such as Satyrs, Centaurs, Great Eagles, and Rogues to fight alongside them.

The High Men

General: High Men are tall, pale-skinned beings believed to have descended from the heavens. Most are taller than the average Human, but with less individual variations in appearance. High Men project a serious demeanor and seem to have a very limited sense of humor. They are highly respected by the good beings, while many of the neutrals and evil beings view them with distrust and suspicion.

Society: High Men society is built upon a foundation of strict order and purity. High Men participate in few forms of entertainment and relish tranquil relaxation above more earthly pleasures. It is thought that the High Men spend most of their time protecting the world from evil, especially the Undead, but they are rarely seen away from the battlefield, and the other races know little about them.

Combat: The High Men are a magical race by nature and rely heavily on their supernatural abilities in combat. They fight most effectively against their archenemies, the Undead, but fare well against most other races also. With the aid of the Valkyries, Holy Avengers, Titans and Astra, the High Men are able to hold their ground and continue fighting against the powerful forces of evil.

The Azracs

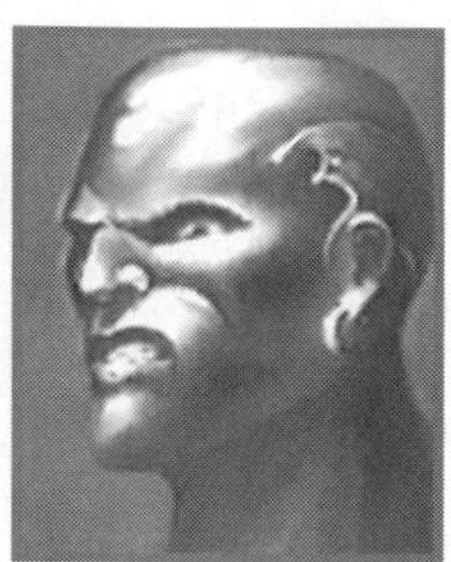

General: The Azracs are an aggressive, desert-dwelling race. They are, in many ways, similar to Humans. What little hair they have on their bodies they usually shave. Azracs wear minimal clothing and disdain heavy armor. Their religious zeal makes them particularly aggressive and fanatic.

Society: Azrac society is one of strict religious and societal conformity. Insubordination to one's superiors is neither tolerated nor punished lightly. Azracs believe that the almighty god, Yaka, ordains one's social status. Still, a high level of respect for all other Azracs is common in Azrac society.

Azracs are wary of most races and only ally themselves with other neutral races, unless truly dire circumstances force them to broaden the scope of their trust. They typically do not mix or intermingle even with their allies, as all others are seen as inferior in the eyes of Yaka. Azracs disdain the concepts of good and evil, and will go to war with any who stand in the way of their religious beliefs or goals.

Combat: Azracs will fight fearlessly, because they believe that dying for their god will make them immortal. They are prepared to give their lives for their king or god at any time. In combat, Azracs most often take the offensive and attack relentlessly. They are naturally good fighters because of their inbred toughness, fostered by living in a harsh desert environment. Their disdain for any kind of armor leaves them somewhat vulnerable, however. Azrac tactics typically consist of overrunning their enemies with brute force and magic, and they rarely employ stealth tactics.

The Frostlings

General: Frostlings are a race of small, nomadic humanoids that dwell in the cold northern regions. They are thought to be distant relatives of the Goblins. Frostlings possess a gray complexion and large, deep-blue eyes. Frostling clothing is simple and often weather-worn from the harsh cold winds and ice storms. Because of their natural resistance to the cold, however, Frostlings need little protection from the wintry elements.

Society: Frostling society embraces hard work and struggle. Because of the harsh environment and weather conditions in which they live, Frostlings must rely extensively on the cooperation and support of their fellow townsfolk and neighboring communities.

As a nomadic people, when the weather becomes unbearable, they move south to more temperate climates. Oftentimes, the Frostlings will put together raiding parties to conquer nearby towns when they need shelter from extremely harsh weather.

Combat: Frostlings are a hardy race, but they are not known for their fighting ability. They are still feared on the battlefield, however, because of the allies they bring from the north, including Dire Penguins, Yeti, Frost Queens, and Ice Drakes. Frostlings rely on fighting ability, magic, and sheer numbers to overcome their foes, utilizing a wider array of tactics when in their home terrain. As a result, their ability to expand their home terrain makes them even more dangerous.

The Humans

General: The most common inhabitant of the land is man. The youngest of the races, Humans have only been present in the land with the other ancient races for a few centuries. Still, Humans have spread across all parts of the land and have become varied in appearance and nature. Their adaptability allows them to live and thrive in nearly any climate.

Society: Due to their relatively short life spans, Humans tend to strive to accomplish things as quickly as possible. Their cities have risen from the ground to encompass vast stretches of land. Human rulers claim dominion over huge empires and believe they are destined to dominate the entire world. These rugged people can adapt to any climate and can even live underground. Humans seem to be making incredible advances in technology in recent times, accelerating their spread across the lands.

Combat: Humans have been known to use a wide array of combat tactics against other races, depending on the nature of the enemy. Humans make average warriors, clerics, archers and cavalry. Mounted knights make a very strong addition to cavalry, and charlatans are often used for sneak attacks or ranged support. The preferred weapon of almost all Human warriors is the long sword. When available, Human musketeers can give a decided advantage in town sieges and ranged attacks.

The Lizardmen

General: Lizardmen are a savage race of reptilian humanoids. Lizardmen are covered in scales and vary in color from deep green to a lighter brown-green. Lizardmen prefer to live near large bodies of water or swamps, but can thrive in nearly any climate except the cold North.

Society: Lizardmen society is governed almost entirely by strength and brute force. All Lizardmen answer to a single king, selected by his ability to defeat the current king in hand-to-hand combat. One's status in determined almost entirely at or before birth. Potential Heroes and kings usually have some discerning characteristic present on their eggs, or on their bodies once hatched. A spotted egg often forecasts the birth of a shaman or one with magical ability.

Since magic is viewed with distrust in Lizardmen society, a close eye is kept on those few shamans with the ability to wield magical powers. Still, they are typically given important roles, such as becoming the king's advisors or the town's healers.

Combat: In combat, Lizardmen fight in unorganized groups, relying heavily on frontal assaults. Lizardmen are extremely aggressive and prefer melee combat to missile attacks. One of their most devastating tactics is to cross bodies of water and launch surprise attacks on unsuspecting cities. They are able to do so with full siege weaponry, as they employ specially constructed ballistas and catapults mounted atop giant turtles.

The Dark Elves

General: Dark Elves are the evil counterparts of normal Elves. They prefer to live in darkness, hidden from the sun's revealing rays. Although they were once part of the Elven community that walks in the glow of the sun, they choose now to live underground. After only a few generations, they began adapting to the darkness and disliking the sunlight. Most Dark Elves have a dark gray-green complexion with white or silver hair.

Society: The Dark Elves once enjoyed the same life of peace and relaxation as their kindred Elves on the surface. Now, their lives are filled with chaos and disaster, much of which is brought on by living underground. Still, the Dark Elves strive to achieve order through their strict family caste system. Most Dark Elves are too preoccupied with their lust for vengeance against the Humans and other Elves to relax during rare periods of peace and quiet.

Combat: Dark Elves will use any means necessary to achieve victory in battle. Although their warriors and archers are just as skilled as those of the Elves, the Dark Elves tend to rely on tactics involving deception and surprise. Most often, they will achieve these effects through the use of magic—which they are able to master easily—drawing power from dark rituals and necromancy. Oftentimes, when a direct assault is needed, they will send in allied Orcs and Goblins to thin the ranks of the enemy before sending their elite Executioners.

The Goblins

General: Related to the Orcs, these little horrors live in filthy underground tunnels. They are feared, not for their strength, but for their multitude. Goblins hate bright sunlight and will try to avoid it. Goblins are often characterized as stupid creatures, probably because of the number of times that they have been duped and enslaved by other races. While not a particularly smart race, Goblins are quite technically proficient, and have been known to replicate and modify existing designs and creations to suit their malicious needs.

Society: Goblins mostly live in tribes underground. Their holes are filthy breeding grounds for a wide variety of diseases, none of which seem to affect them. Goblin society is one of struggle and war in which every member of society must contribute. Most Goblins live almost entirely for the thrill of the carnage they cause and the loot they capture. Rarely will one ever witness a Goblin performing physical labor of its own free will. Goblins tend to have a wicked, cruel streak, and common forms of entertainment include torturing prisoners and gladiatorial fights between captives, beasts, or any mix thereof.

Combat: Goblins are not particularly strong in combat, and they tend to use nontraditional weaponry such as spears, poisonous darts, and bombs to gain the upper hand. Often thought to be stupid creatures, Goblins are frequently able to use this very stereotype to their advantage in battle, employing a variety of unconventional, but effective, battle tactics. Still, more often than not, Goblins achieve their battle victories through overwhelming numbers alone.

The Orcs

General: Orcs are a race of humanoids known for their rough facial features and brutality in battle. They stand roughly as tall as Humans, their hair is typically dark and unkempt, and their skin tone is a greenish hue. Orcs are not thought to be very intelligent beings, but are well-respected and feared in battle by both allies and enemies.

Society: Orcs believe that they are the supreme race. They have little, if any, respect for other races. Pride, wealth, and territory are highly valued, and Orcs believe the best way to obtain these things is through war and battle. Orc society is harsh. Its members are forced to endure many types of pain, suffering, and deprivation on a daily basis in order to make them stronger. Status is based solely on one's rank within the military, which is usually based on strength and stamina. When not at war, Orcs often fight amongst each other for lack of any other way to express their aggression.

Combat: Orcs take particular pleasure in the brutality of war and hand-to-hand combat. They have refined the art of war to a degree beyond that of any other race and are able to deal with almost any situation through some means of force, be it by combat or assassination. Since not every Orc is cut out for infantry, much less cavalry and the elite ranks, ranks of archers and shamans are plentiful, although they are rarely ever called upon except when tactically needed. Orcs consider the use of magic in battle cowardly, and one of the only reasons an Orc will ever run from battle is if the enemy is utilizing magic heavily.

The Undead

General: The masses of Undead found their way to the land of the living through a planar rift, opened when the Trumps of Doom were sounded. Now that they are among the living, they seek solely to destroy all living creatures and add them to their soulless ranks. The most common type of Undead appear as skeletal remains of their once living bodies. However, other types of Undead exist as well, including Wraiths and the dreaded Reaper.

Society: Undead have little "society" of which to speak. They often conquer and occupy the towns and cities of other races. Some Undead are needed to do basic work to maintain the housing and buildings in these cities, but most Undead exist only to destroy everything else around them and expand the numbers and reach of their people.

Combat: Already dead, Undead have little to fear. They can be destroyed most often by brute force, but most are immune to the effects of poison and fear and are highly resistant to lightning, fire and cold. Slow moving and expendable, Undead often resort to victory by numbers. Expecting such tactics, many a town has been surprised and overrun by more powerful Wraiths or by swift-moving Demons, Hellhounds, and Werewolves.

Appendix 1
Units and Spells

Extended Unit Statistics

When examining a Unit, you also see several other statistics. These also play a VERY important role in choosing the best unit for different situations. For instance, if you need to get a lot of units quickly, but do not have very much gold, you should go for Tier 1 Units since they tend to cost the least and have the lowest upkeep. Each statistic of a unit can have a profound impact upon how you field your combat forces.

Race

The race of a unit affects how friendly they will be to you. For instance, if you are the Dwarves and are at war with the Orcs, but have good racial relations with the Elves, independent Elves will tend to want to join you, while Orcs will want to fight you. If you are Neutral towards the Humans, yet you attack them, your racial relations with them will slowly dissolve, and they might declare war on you. It is very important to make sure that when you attack a Unit, you know whether you want good or bad diplomatic relations with that Race.

Alignment

The Alignment of a Unit, and how you treat that Unit, also affects your diplomatic relations with that Unit. Good units tend to align themselves with other Good Units, while Evil units tend to fight Good Units. The Alignment of a unit can affect the likelihood that they will join with you.

Experience

Experience is displayed by a fraction with the Numerator representing the current experience that the unit has gained, and the Denominator representing the amount of experience that the unit needs to achieve either experienced or veteran status. Unlike Heroes, Units can only gain 2 'levels'. A silver medallion denotes experienced Units, and a gold medallion denotes Veteran Units.

Level

The level of a unit is a number between 1 and 4, and is a rough estimate of how strong the unit is. Usually you want to match the Level of your forces to the Level of your enemies' forces; however, it is ideal to exceed theirs. Level 1 units can generally be produced at level one cities, level 2 units at level 2 cities, etc.

Upkeep

This represents the cost for food and supplies for any given unit. Upper-tier units require more upkeep than lower-tier units.

Extended Unit Information

Extended Unit Statistics

The following lists every unit that can be built by the 12 races. While there are other units in the game that can be summoned or found, this list focuses solely on the playable races. The list contains a picture of the unit, for easy reference, as well as the unit's Name, Type, Level, Cost, Attack, Defense, Movement, Damage, Resistance, and Hit Points. Please note that the following abbreviations have been used.

Level	=	Lvl
Cost	=	Cost
Attack	=	At
Defense	=	Def
Movement	=	Mov
Damage	=	Dam
Resistance	=	Res
Hit Points	=	Hits

On each unit's second line is a list of abilities it has.

Appendix 1 - Race Units

Elves

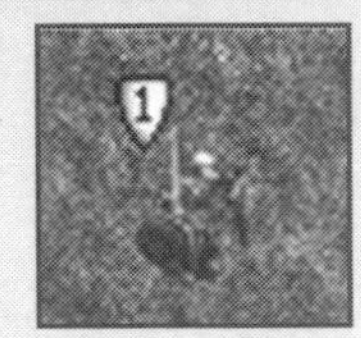

Swordsman

Type	Lvl	Cost	At	Def	Mov	Dam	Res	Hits
Humanoid	1	15	5	2	26	2	4	5

Walking, Forestry, Strike

Nymph

Type	Lvl	Cost	At	Def	Mov	Dam	Res	Hits
Humanoid	1	22	4	1	26	1	5	5

Walking, Forestry, Strike, Seduce

Archer

Type	Lvl	Cost	At	Def	Mov	Dam	Res	Hits
Humanoid	1	17	3	2	26	2	4	5

Walking, Forestry, Archery, Marksmanship 1

Battering Ram

Type	Lvl	Cost	At	Def	Mov	Dam	Res	Hits
Machine	1	23	1	2	20	1	3	10

Walking, Poison Immunity, Fearless, Cold Protection, Wall Crushing

Scout

Type	Lvl	Cost	At	Def	Mov	Dam	Res	Hits
Humanoid	2	32	6	3	36	2	4	7

Walking, Forestry, Strike, Vision 1, Charge

Cleric

Type	Lvl	Cost	At	Def	Mov	Dam	Res	Hits
Humanoid	2	32	3	2	26	2	5	5

Walking, Forestry, Magic Strike, Strike, Turn Undead 1, Entangle, Healing, Dispel magic 1, Magic Bolts

Ballista

Type	Lvl	Cost	At	Def	Mov	Dam	Res	Hits
Machine	2	56	1	2	20	1	3	7

Walking, Poison Immunity, Shoot Javelin, Fearless, Cold Protection

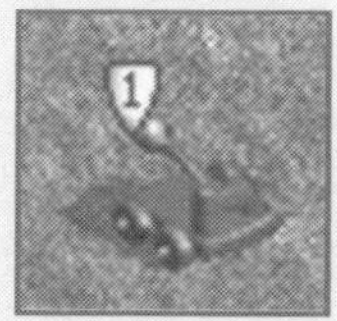

Catapult

Type	Lvl	Cost	At	Def	Mov	Dam	Res	Hits
Machine	2	58	1	2	20	1	3	8

Walking, Poison Immunity, Hurl Boulder, Fearless, Cold Protection

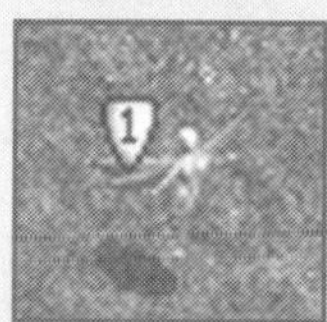

Fairy

Type	Lvl	Cost	At	Def	Mov	Dam	Res	Hits
Creature	3	55	3	5	32	3	6	6

Flying, Magic Strike, Strike, Concealment

Unicorn

Type	Lvl	Cost	At	Def	Mov	Dam	Res	Hits
Creature	3	90	6	4	36	4	8	10

Walking, Forestry, Magic Strike, Strike, Healing, Charge

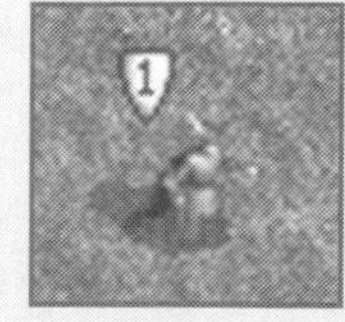

Ranger

Type	Lvl	Cost	At	Def	Mov	Dam	Res	Hits
Humanoid	3	95	5	3	26	3	5	8

Walking, Swimming, Forestry, Mountaineering, Strike, Archery, Marksmanship 2, Concealment

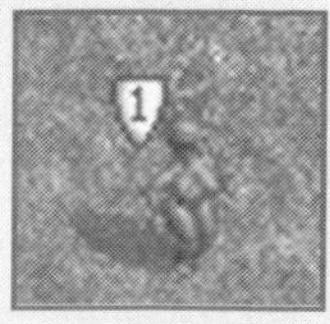

Nature Elemental

Type	Lvl	Cost	At	Def	Mov	Dam	Res	Hits
Creature	4	210	5	7	32	5	8	15

Walking, Forestry, Poison Immunity, Strike, Entangle, Regeneration, Path of Life, Fire Protection, Lightning Protection, Cold Protection

Halflings

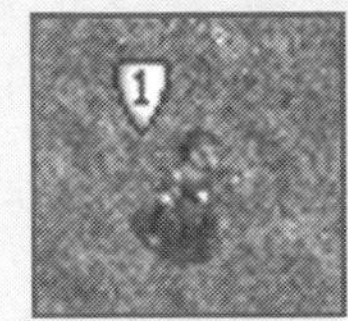

Slinger

Type	Lvl	Cost	At	Def	Mov	Dam	Res	Hits
Humanoid	1	15	3	2	24	2	4	5

Walking, Hurl Stones

Pony Rider

Type	Lvl	Cost	At	Def	Mov	Dam	Res	Hits
Humanoid	1	28	5	2	32	3	4	7

Walking, Strike, Charge

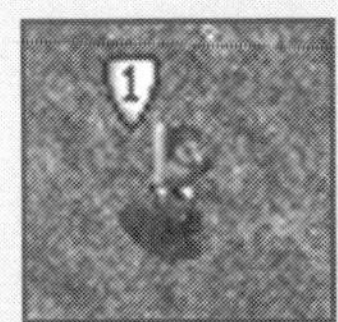

Swordsman

Type	Lvl	Cost	At	Def	Mov	Dam	Res	Hits
Humanoid	1	14	4	2	24	2	4	5

Walking, Strike, Parry

Battering Ram

Type	Lvl	Cost	At	Def	Mov	Dam	Res	Hits
Machine	1	23	1	2	20	1	3	10

Walking, Poison Immunity, Fearless, Cold Protection, Wall Crushing

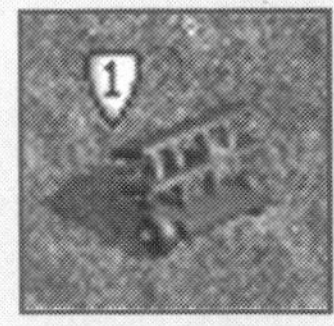

Ballista

Type	Lvl	Cost	At	Def	Mov	Dam	Res	Hits
Machine	2	56	1	2	20	1	3	7

Walking, Poison Immunity, Shoot Javelin, Fearless, Cold Protection

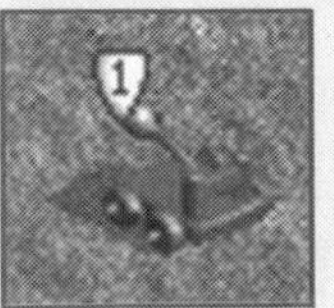

Catapult

Type	Lvl	Cost	At	Def	Mov	Dam	Res	Hits
Machine	2	58	1	2	20	1	3	8

Walking, Poison Immunity, Hurl Boulder, Fearless, Cold Protection

Cleric

Type	Lvl	Cost	At	Def	Mov	Dam	Res	Hits
Humanoid	2	30	3	2	24	2	5	5

Walking, Magic Strike, Strike, Turn Undead 1, Healing, Dispel Magic 1, Magic Protection, Magic Bolts

Satyr

Type	Lvl	Cost	At	Def	Mov	Dam	Res	Hits
Creature	2	35	4	2	26	3	6	6

Walking, Forestry, Strike, Bard's Skills, Charm

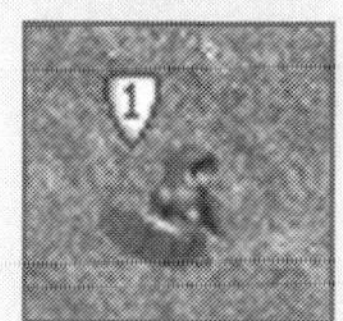

Rogue

Type	Lvl	Cost	At	Def	Mov	Dam	Res	Hits
Humanoid	3	75	5	4	26	4	4	6

Walking, Strike, Hurl Stones, Marksmanship 1, Wall Climbing, Concealment

Centaur

Type	Lvl	Cost	At	Def	Mov	Dam	Res	Hits
Creature	3	80	6	3	36	3	6	11

Walking, Forestry, Strike, Archery, Marksmanship 2, Charge

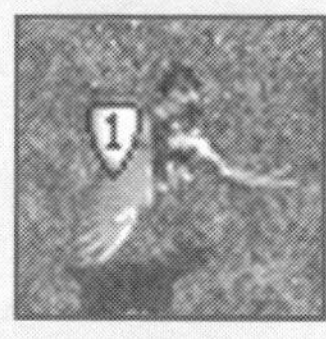

Eagle Rider

Type	Lvl	Cost	At	Def	Mov	Dam	Res	Hits
Humanoid	3	55	5	2	36	4	4	8

Flying, Strike, Vision 2, Charge

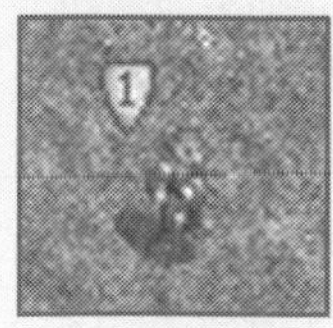

Leprechaun

Type	Lvl	Cost	At	Def	Mov	Dam	Res	Hits
Humanoid	4	190	5	10	26	3	10	7

Walking, Forestry, Magic Strike, Strike, Regeneration, Invisibility, Dispel Magic 1, Fearless, Death Protection, Poison Protection, Parry, Magic Bolts

Dwarves

Battering Ram

Type	Lvl	Cost	At	Def	Mov	Dam	Res	Hits
Machine	1	23	1	2	20	1	3	10

Walking, Poison Immunity, Fearless, Cold Protection, Wall Crushing

Berserker

Type	Lvl	Cost	At	Def	Mov	Dam	Res	Hits
Humanoid	1	17	4	1	24	4	4	6

Walking, Mountaineering, Strike, Fearless, Poison Protection, Round Attack

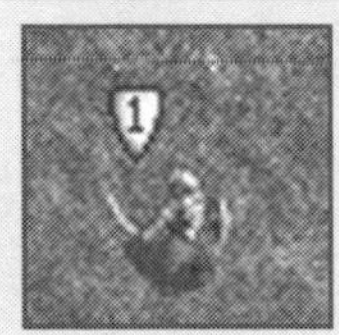

Axeman

Type	Lvl	Cost	At	Def	Mov	Dam	Res	Hits
Humanoid	1	16	4	2	24	3	4	5

Walking, Cave Crawling, Mountaineering, Strike, Poison Protection

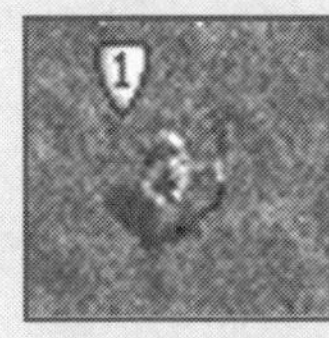

Archer

Type	Lvl	Cost	At	Def	Mov	Dam	Res	Hits
Humanoid	1	16	5	2	24	3	4	5

Walking, Cave Crawling, Mountaineering, Archery, Poison Protection

Boar Rider

Type	Lvl	Cost	At	Def	Mov	Dam	Res	Hits
Humanoid	2	36	5	2	32	3	4	8

Walking, Mountaineering, Strike, Poison Protection, Charge

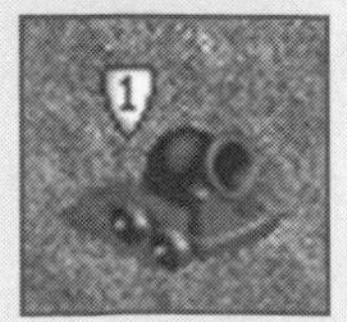

Bombardier

Type	Lvl	Cost	At	Def	Mov	Dam	Res	Hits
Machine	2	79	1	2	20	1	3	10

Walking, Poison Immunity, Fire Cannon, Fearless, Cold Protection

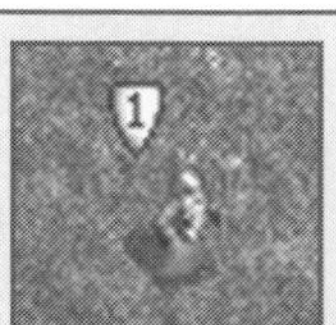

Cleric

Type	Lvl	Cost	At	Def	Mov	Dam	Res	Hits
Humanoid	2	35	3	2	24	2	5	5

Walking, Cave Crawling, Mountaineering, Magic Strike, Strike, Turn Undead 1, Healing, Dispel Magic 1, Fearless, Poison Protection, Magic Bolts

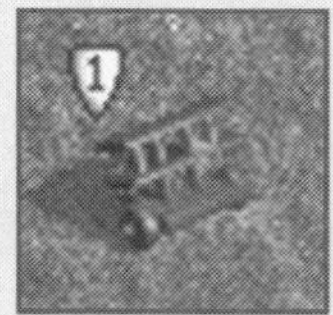

Ballista

Type	Lvl	Cost	At	Def	Mov	Dam	Res	Hits
Machine	2	56	1	2	20	1	3	7

Walking, Poison Immunity, Shoot Javelin, Fearless, Cold Protection

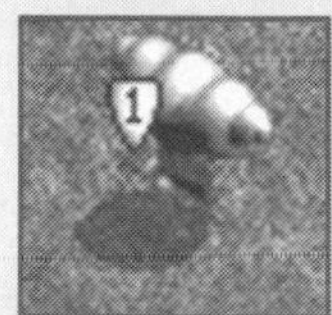

Balloon

Type	Lvl	Cost	At	Def	Mov	Dam	Res	Hits
Machine	3	55	2	2	32	8	3	12

Flying, Poison Immunity, Vision 3

Mole

Type	Lvl	Cost	At	Def	Mov	Dam	Res	Hits
Machine	3	105	5	3	32	4	4	14

Cave Crawling, Mountaineering, Strike, Night Vision, Tunneling, Poison Protection, Wall Crushing

Giant

Type	Lvl	Cost	At	Def	Mov	Dam	Res	Hits
Humanoid	3	105	6	3	32	7	4	15

Walking, Mountaineering, Strike, Hurl Boulder

Dwarf Firstborn

Type	Lvl	Cost	At	Def	Mov	Dam	Res	Hits
Humanoid	4	205	7	5	24	7	6	24

Walking, Mountaineering, Fire Immunity, Poison Immunity, Fire Strike, Strike, Fearless, Magic Protection

High Men

Spirit Puppet

Type	Lvl	Cost	At	Def	Mov	Dam	Res	Hits
Creature	1	20	4	2	30	2	4	4

Walking, Cold Immunity, Lightning Immunity, Poison Immunity, Death Immunity, Holy Immunity, Magic Strike, Strike, Magic Protection

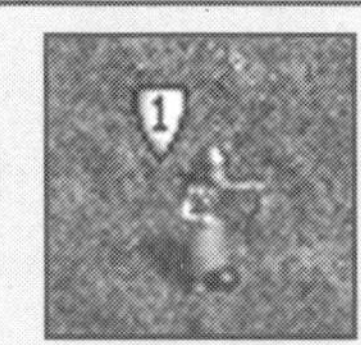

Archer

Type	Lvl	Cost	At	Def	Mov	Dam	Res	Hits
Humanoid	1	15	3	2	30	1	4	5

Walking, Archery, True Seeing, Holy Protection

Swordsman

Type	Lvl	Cost	At	Def	Mov	Dam	Res	Hits
Humanoid	1	15	4	2	30	3	4	5

Walking, Strike, True Seeing, Holy Protection

Battering Ram

Type	Lvl	Cost	At	Def	Mov	Dam	Res	Hits
Machine	1	23	1	2	20	1	3	10

Walking, Poison Immunity, Fearless, Cold Protection, Wall Crushing

Saint

Type	Lvl	Cost	At	Def	Mov	Dam	Res	Hits
Humanoid	2	40	3	2	30	2	5	5

Walking, Holy Strike, Magic Strike, Strike, Turn Undead 2, True Seeing, Healing, Dispel Magic 1, Holy Protection, Holy Bolts, Charm

Paladin

Type	Lvl	Cost	At	Def	Mov	Dam	Res	Hits
Humanoid	2	46	5	3	40	3	5	8

Walking, Strike, Turn Undead 1, True Seeing, Healing, Holy Protection, Charge

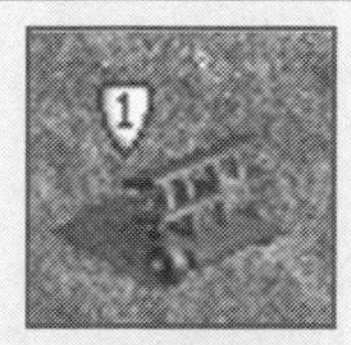

Ballista

Type	Lvl	Cost	At	Def	Mov	Dam	Res	Hits
Machine	2	56	1	2	20	1	3	7

Walking, Poison Immunity, Shoot Javelin, Fearless, Cold Protection

Catapult

Type	Lvl	Cost	At	Def	Mov	Dam	Res	Hits
Machine	2	58	1	2	20	1	3	8

Walking, Poison Immunity, Hurl Boulder, Fearless, Cold Protection

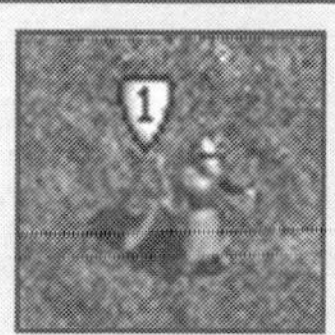

Avenger

Type	Lvl	Cost	At	Def	Mov	Dam	Res	Hits
Humanoid	3	75	5	4	32	3	7	7

Walking, Swimming, Forestry, Cave Crawling, Mountaineering, Death Immunity, Holy Immunity, Holy Strike, Magic Strike, Strike, Turn Undead 2, True Seeing, Fearless, Holy Bolts, Holy Champion

Valkyrie

Type	Lvl	Cost	At	Def	Mov	Dam	Res	Hits
Creature	3	85	7	4	36	3	5	8

Flying, Holy Immunity, Holy Strike, Strike, Vision 2, Fearless, Charge

Titan

Type	Lvl	Cost	At	Def	Mov	Dam	Res	Hits
Creature	3	105	6	5	36	6	5	15

Walking, Fire Immunity, Strike, Holy Protection, Round Attack, First Strike

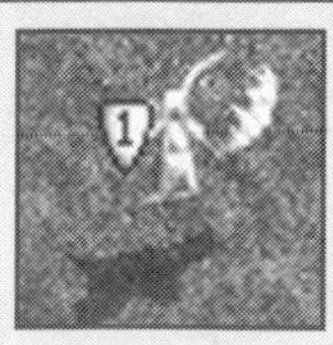

Astra

Type	Lvl	Cost	At	Def	Mov	Dam	Res	Hits
Creature	4	200	7	4	36	6	8	20

Flying, Holy Immunity, Fire Strike, Strike, True Seeing, Healing, Dispel Magic 1, Vision 2, Fearless, Fire Protection

Humans

Pikeman

Type	Lvl	Cost	At	Def	Mov	Dam	Res	Hits
Humanoid	1	17	4	2	26	3	3	5

Walking, Strike, First Strike

Swordsman

Type	Lvl	Cost	At	Def	Mov	Dam	Res	Hits
Humanoid	1	15	4	2	26	3	3	5

Walking, Strike

Archer

Type	Lvl	Cost	At	Def	Mov	Dam	Res	Hits
Humanoid	1	15	3	2	26	2	3	5

Walking, Archery

Battering Ram

Type	Lvl	Cost	At	Def	Mov	Dam	Res	Hits
Machine	1	23	1	2	20	1	3	10

Walking, Poison Immunity, Fearless, Cold Protection, Wall Crushing

Priest

Type	Lvl	Cost	At	Def	Mov	Dam	Res	Hits
Humanoid	2	30	3	2	26	2	4	5

Walking, Magic Strike, Strike, Turn Undead 1, Healing, Dispel Magic 1, Magic Bolts

Medium Cavalry

Type	Lvl	Cost	At	Def	Mov	Dam	Res	Hits
Humanoid	2	35	5	3	26	3	3	8

Walking, Strike, Charge

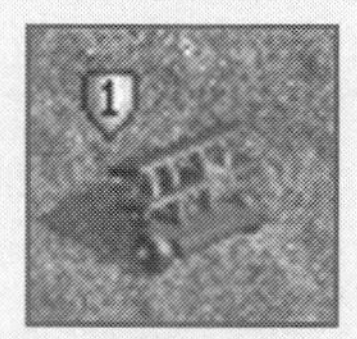

Ballista

Type	Lvl	Cost	At	Def	Mov	Dam	Res	Hits
Machine	2	56	1	2	20	1	3	7

Walking, Poison Immunity, Shoot Javelin, Fearless, Cold Protection

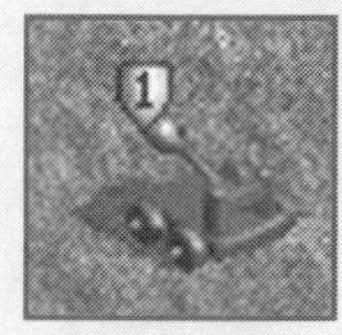

Catapult

Type	Lvl	Cost	At	Def	Mov	Dam	Res	Hits
Machine	2	58	1	2	20	1	3	8

Walking, Poison Immunity, Hurl Boulder, Fearless, Cold Protection

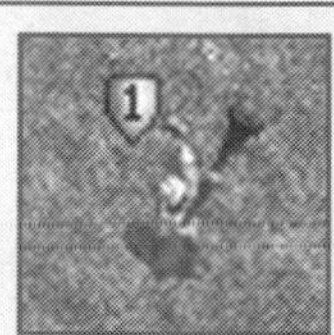

Musketeer

Type	Lvl	Cost	At	Def	Mov	Dam	Res	Hits
Humanoid	3	45	3	2	26	2	3	5

Walking, Fire Musket

Charlatan

Type	Lvl	Cost	At	Def	Mov	Dam	Res	Hits
Humanoid	3	75	4	3	26	3	5	7

Walking, Strike, Bard's Skills, Magic Bolts, Concealment, Charm

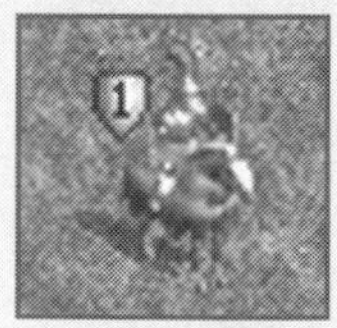

Cavalier

Type	Lvl	Cost	At	Def	Mov	Dam	Res	Hits
Humanoid	3	95	6	6	36	4	4	12

Walking, Strike, Fearless, Charge, Parry

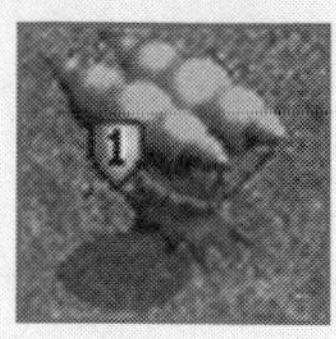

Air Galley

Type	Lvl	Cost	At	Def	Mov	Dam	Res	Hits
Machine	4	230	6	6	32	5	5	18

Flying, Poison Immunity, Marksmanship 1, Shoot Javelin, Vision 1, Fearless, Cold Protection

Azracs

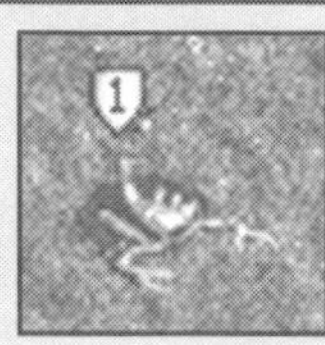

Scorpion

Type	Lvl	Cost	At	Def	Mov	Dam	Res	Hits
Creature	1	15	3	3	24	3	2	5

Walking, Poison Immunity, Poison Strike, Strike, Fire Protection

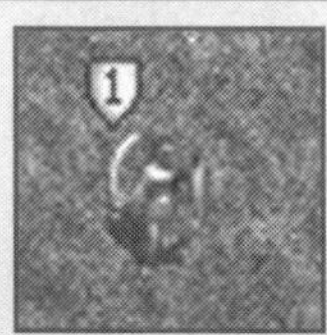

Swordsman

Type	Lvl	Cost	At	Def	Mov	Dam	Res	Hits
Humanoid	1	15	5	1	26	4	3	5

Walking, Strike, Fire Protection

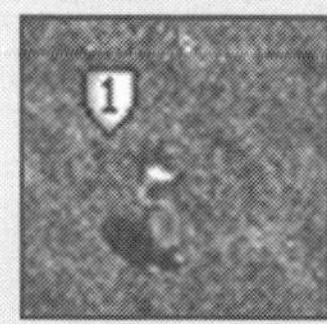

Archer

Type	Lvl	Cost	At	Def	Mov	Dam	Res	Hits
Humanoid	1	15	3	1	26	2	3	5

Walking, Archery, Fire Protection

Elephant

Type	Lvl	Cost	At	Def	Mov	Dam	Res	Hits
Creature	1	37	4	3	30	4	3	12

Walking, Strike, Wall Crushing

Priest

Type	Lvl	Cost	At	Def	Mov	Dam	Res	Hits
Humanoid	2	30	3	1	26	2	4	5

Walking, Fire Immunity, Magic Strike, Strike, Turn Undead 1, Healing, Dispel Magic 1, Magic Bolts

Rider

Type	Lvl	Cost	At	Def	Mov	Dam	Res	Hits
Humanoid	2	36	5	3	40	3	3	8

Walking, Strike, Fire Protection, Charge

Ballista

Type	Lvl	Cost	At	Def	Mov	Dam	Res	Hits
Machine	2	56	1	2	20	1	3	7

Walking, Poison Immunity, Shoot Javelin, Fearless, Cold Protection

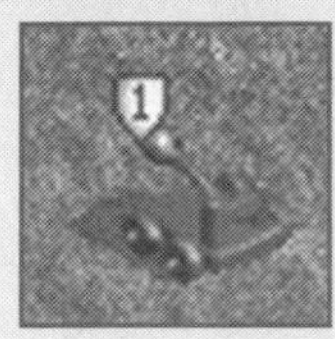

Catapult

Type	Lvl	Cost	At	Def	Mov	Dam	Res	Hits
Machine	2	58	1	2	20	1	3	8

Walking, Poison Immunity, Hurl Boulder, Fearless, Cold Protection

Sand Worm

Type	Lvl	Cost	At	Def	Mov	Dam	Res	Hits
Creature	3	65	4	3	26	5	4	12

Walking, Cave Crawling, Strike, Tunneling, Fire Protection, Desert Concealment, Fire Strike

Djinn

Type	Lvl	Cost	At	Def	Mov	Dam	Res	Hits
Creature	3	68	5	4	32	4	6	10

Magic Strike, Strike, Floating, Magic Bolts

Beholder

Type	Lvl	Cost	At	Def	Mov	Dam	Res	Hits
Creature	3	106	5	3	24	3	6	15

Strike, Night Vision, True Seeing, Cause Fear, Doom Gaze, Floating, Vision 1

Yaka Avatar

Type	Lvl	Cost	At	Def	Mov	Dam	Res	Hits
Creature	4	200	8	5	32	6	8	20

Walking, Fire Immunity, Magic Strike, Strike, Dominate, Vision 2, Fearless, Magic Bolts

Lizardmen

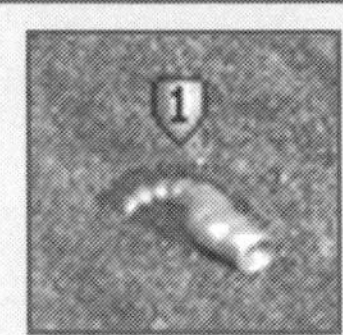

Giant Slug

Type	Lvl	Cost	At	Def	Mov	Dam	Res	Hits
Creature	1	12	3	1	20	3	2	5

Walking, Cave Crawling, Poison Strike, Strike, Venomous Spit, Poison Protection

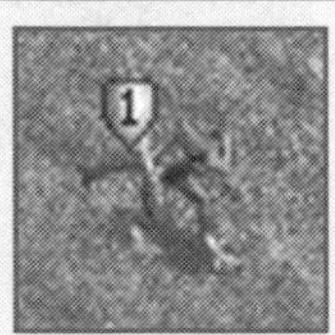

Swordsman

Type	Lvl	Cost	At	Def	Mov	Dam	Res	Hits
Humanoid	1	15	4	2	26	3	2	5

Walking, Swimming, Strike

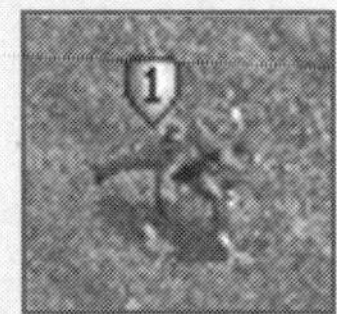

Archer

Type	Lvl	Cost	At	Def	Mov	Dam	Res	Hits
Humanoid	1	15	3	2	26	2	2	5

Walking, Swimming, Archery

Battering Ram

Type	Lvl	Cost	At	Def	Mov	Dam	Res	Hits
Machine	1	23	1	2	20	1	3	10

Walking, Poison Immunity, Fearless, Cold Protection, Wall Crushing

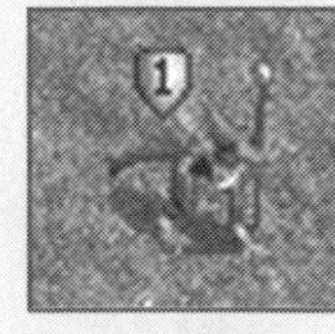

Shaman

Type	Lvl	Cost	At	Def	Mov	Dam	Res	Hits
Humanoid	2	30	3	2	26	2	3	5

Walking, Swimming, Magic Strike, Strike, Turn Undead 1, Healing, Dispel Magic 1, Poison Protection, Magic Bolts

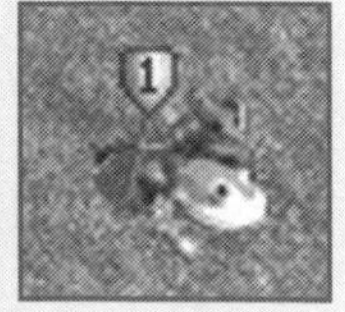

Frog Rider

Type	Lvl	Cost	At	Def	Mov	Dam	Res	Hits
Humanoid	2	35	5	3	32	3	2	7

Walking, Swimming, Strike, Charge

Turtle Ballista

Type	Lvl	Cost	At	Def	Mov	Dam	Res	Hits
Creature	2	45	6	3	20	5	3	7

Walking, Swimming, Shoot Javelin

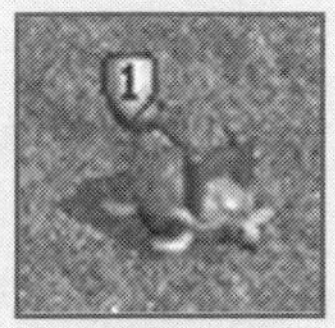

Turtle Catapult

Type	Lvl	Cost	At	Def	Mov	Dam	Res	Hits
Creature	2	50	5	3	20	8	3	8

Walking, Swimming, Hurl Boulder

Lurker

Type	Lvl	Cost	At	Def	Mov	Dam	Res	Hits
Creature	3	65	5	3	24	6	3	10

Walking, Swimming, Poison Strike, Strike, Poison Protection, Water Concealment

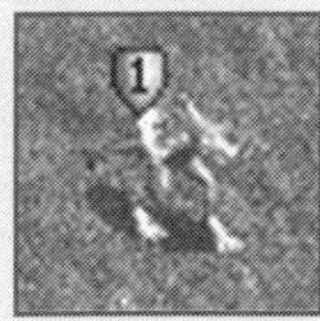

Salamander

Type	Lvl	Cost	At	Def	Mov	Dam	Res	Hits
Creature	3	75	7	4	26	4	5	10

Walking, Fire Immunity, Fire Strike, Strike, Parry

Green Wyvern

Type	Lvl	Cost	At	Def	Mov	Dam	Res	Hits
Creature	3	130	4	4	36	5	6	12

Flying, Poison Immunity, Poison Strike, Strike, Vision 2, Fearless

Basilisk

Type	Lvl	Cost	At	Def	Mov	Dam	Res	Hits
Creature	4	243	7	6	36	5	5	22

Walking, Swimming, Poison Immunity, Strike, Night Vision, True Seeing, Doom Gaze, Fearless

Frostlings

Archer

Type	Lvl	Cost	At	Def	Mov	Dam	Res	Hits
Humanoid	1	15	3	2	24	2	3	5

Walking, Archery, Cold Protection

Dire Penguin

Type	Lvl	Cost	At	Def	Mov	Dam	Res	Hits
Creature	1	15	5	2	24	2	3	5

Walking, Swimming, Strike, Cold Protection

Swordsman

Type	Lvl	Cost	At	Def	Mov	Dam	Res	Hits
Humanoid	1	15	4	2	24	3	3	5

Walking, Strike, Cold Protection

Battering Ram

Type	Lvl	Cost	At	Def	Mov	Dam	Res	Hits
Machine	1	23	1	2	20	1	3	10

Walking, Poison Immunity, Fearless, Cold Protection, Wall Crushing

Ballista

Type	Lvl	Cost	At	Def	Mov	Dam	Res	Hits
Machine	2	56	1	2	20	1	3	7

Walking, Poison Immunity, Shoot Javelin, Fearless, Cold Protection

Wolf Rider

Type	Lvl	Cost	At	Def	Mov	Dam	Res	Hits
Humanoid	2	33	5	3	32	3	3	7

Walking, Forestry, Strike, Cold Protection, Charge

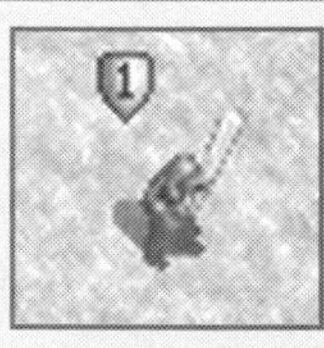

Shaman

Type	Lvl	Cost	At	Def	Mov	Dam	Res	Hits
Humanoid	2	30	3	2	24	2	4	5

Walking, Cold Immunity, Magic Strike, Strike, Turn Undead 1, Healing, Dispel Magic 1, Frost Bolts

Catapult

Type	Lvl	Cost	At	Def	Mov	Dam	Res	Hits
Machine	2	58	1	2	20	1	3	8

Walking, Poison Immunity, Hurl Boulder, Fearless, Cold Protection

Yeti

Type	Lvl	Cost	At	Def	Mov	Dam	Res	Hits
Creature	3	95	6	4	28	6	4	13

Walking, Mountaineering, Cold Immunity, Cold Strike, Strike, Wall Crushing

Frost Queen

Type	Lvl	Cost	At	Def	Mov	Dam	Res	Hits
Humanoid	3	65	4	3	26	3	6	8

Walking, Swimming, Cold Immunity, Cold Strike, Strike, Path of Frost, Frost Bolts, Snow Concealment

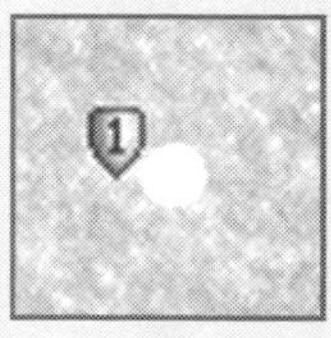

Nordic Glow

Type	Lvl	Cost	At	Def	Mov	Dam	Res	Hits
Creature	3	98	4	5	36	4	6	7

Flying, Fire Immunity, Cold Immunity, Poison Immunity, Magic Strike, Strike, Fearless, Physical Protection

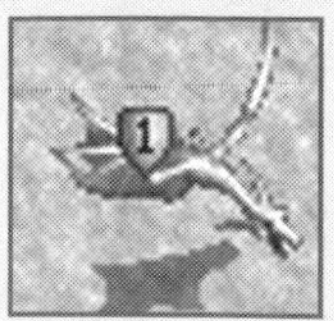

Ice Drake

Type	Lvl	Cost	At	Def	Mov	Dam	Res	Hits
Creature	4	225	7	5	36	4	4	17

Flying, Cold Immunity, Strike, Dragon, Vision 2, Fearless, Cold Breath

Dark Elves

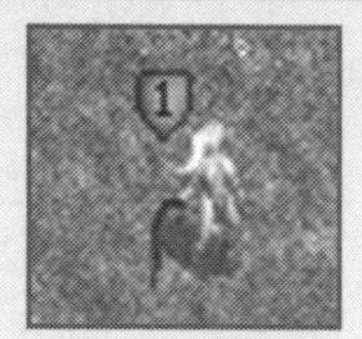

Lady of Pain

Type	Lvl	Cost	At	Def	Mov	Dam	Res	Hits
Humanoid	1	14	4	1	26	2	2	5

Walking, Strike, Seduce

Swordsman

Type	Lvl	Cost	At	Def	Mov	Dam	Res	Hits
Humanoid	1	14	4	2	26	2	5	5

Walking, Strike, Night Vision

Battering Ram

Type	Lvl	Cost	At	Def	Mov	Dam	Res	Hits
Machine	1	23	1	2	20	1	3	10

Walking, Poison Immunity, Fearless, Cold Protection, Wall Crushing

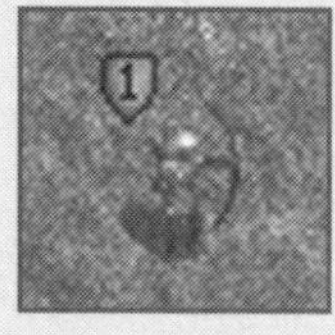

Archer

Type	Lvl	Cost	At	Def	Mov	Dam	Res	Hits
Humanoid	1	17	3	2	26	2	5	5

Walking, Archery, Marksmanship 1, Night Vision

Ballista

Type	Lvl	Cost	At	Def	Mov	Dam	Res	Hits
Machine	2	56	1	2	20	1	3	7

Walking, Poison Immunity, Shoot Javelin, Fearless, Cold Protection

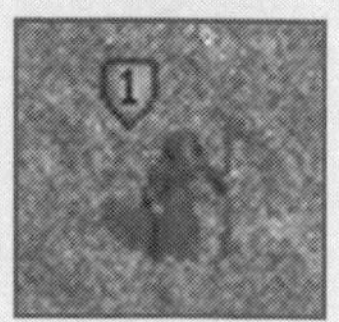

Storm Priest

Type	Lvl	Cost	At	Def	Mov	Dam	Res	Hits
Humanoid	2	32	3	2	26	2	6	5

Walking, Magic Strike, Strike, Turn Undead 1, Night Vision, Healing, Dispel Magic 1, Lightning Protection, Lightning Bolts

Rider

Type	Lvl	Cost	At	Def	Mov	Dam	Res	Hits
Humanoid	2	32	5	3	36	2	5	7

Walking, Strike, Night Vision, Charge

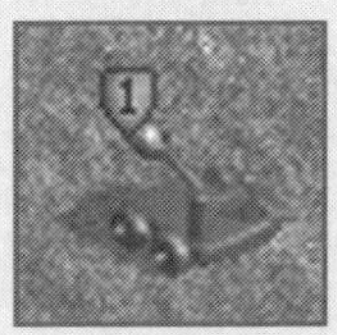

Catapult

Type	Lvl	Cost	At	Def	Mov	Dam	Res	Hits
Machine	2	58	1	2	20	1	3	8

Walking, Poison Immunity, Hurl Boulder, Fearless, Cold Protection

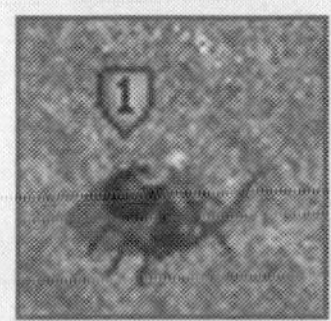

Spider Queen

Type	Lvl	Cost	At	Def	Mov	Dam	Res	Hits
Creature	3	70	4	3	36	4	6	8

Walking, Cave Crawling, Poison Immunity, Poison Strike, Strike, Web, Seduce, Wall Climbing, Night Vision, Magic Bolts

Executioner

Type	Lvl	Cost	At	Def	Mov	Dam	Res	Hits
Humanoid	3	105	7	4	36	4	6	10

Walking, Strike, Trail of Darkness, Night Vision, Fearless, Charge, Life Stealing

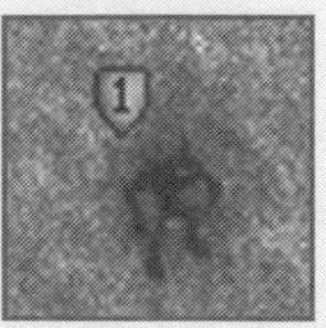

Shadow

Type	Lvl	Cost	At	Def	Mov	Dam	Res	Hits
Creature	3	95	5	4	26	4	5	7

Walking, Cold Immunity, Poison Immunity, Death Immunity, Strike, Night Vision, Cause Fear, Pass Wall, Fearless, Concealment

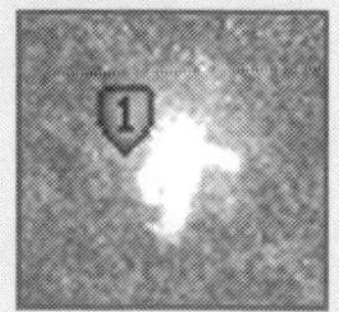

Incarnate

Type	Lvl	Cost	At	Def	Mov	Dam	Res	Hits
Creature	4	200	2	5	36	1	5	10

Fire Immunity, Cold Immunity, Lightning Immunity, Poison Immunity, Death Immunity, Physical Immunity, Magic Strike, Strike, Floating, Possess

Goblins

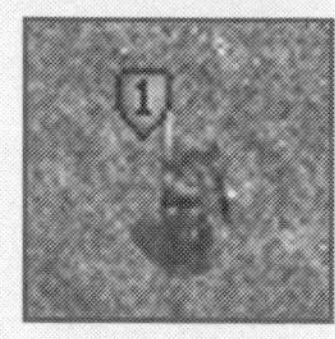

Spearman

Type	Lvl	Cost	At	Def	Mov	Dam	Res	Hits
Humanoid	1	12	4	2	24	2	2	4

Walking, Cave Crawling, Strike, Night Vision, Poison Protection

Darter

Type	Lvl	Cost	At	Def	Mov	Dam	Res	Hits
Humanoid	1	11	3	2	24	2	2	5

Walking, Cave Crawling, Night Vision, Poison Darts, Poison Protection

Battering Ram

Type	Lvl	Cost	At	Def	Mov	Dam	Res	Hits
Machine	1	23	1	2	20	1	3	10

Walking, Poison Immunity, Fearless, Cold Protection, Wall Crushing

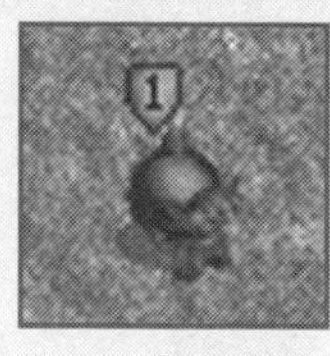

Bomber

Type	Lvl	Cost	At	Def	Mov	Dam	Res	Hits
Humanoid	1	11	3	1	24	2	2	4

Walking, Cave Crawling, Night Vision, Self Destruct, Poison Protection

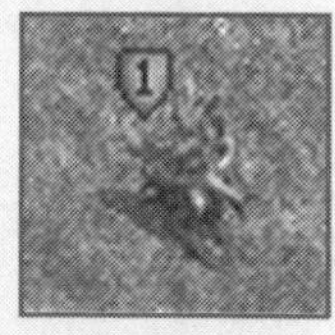

Wolf Rider

Type	Lvl	Cost	At	Def	Mov	Dam	Res	Hits
Humanoid	2	28	5	3	32	3	2	7

Walking, Forestry, Strike, Night Vision, Poison Protection, Charge

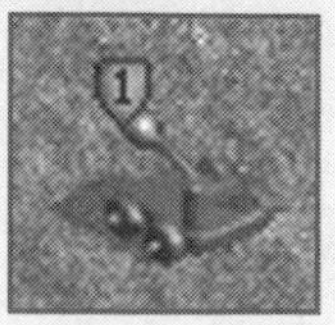

Catapult

Type	Lvl	Cost	At	Def	Mov	Dam	Res	Hits
Machine	2	58	1	2	20	1	3	8

Walking, Poison Immunity, Hurl Boulder, Fearless, Cold Protection

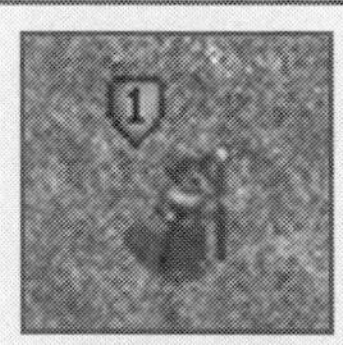

Shaman

Type	Lvl	Cost	At	Def	Mov	Dam	Res	Hits
Humanoid	2	26	3	2	24	2	3	4

Walking, Cave Crawling, Poison Immunity, Magic Strike, Strike, Turn Undead 1, Night Vision, Healing, Dispel Magic 1, Magic Bolts

Ballista

Type	Lvl	Cost	At	Def	Mov	Dam	Res	Hits
Machine	2	56	1	2	20	1	3	7

Walking, Poison Immunity, Shoot Javelin, Fearless, Cold Protection

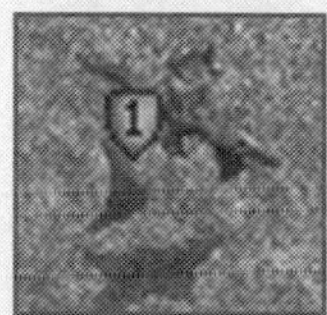

Wyvern Rider

Type	Lvl	Cost	At	Def	Mov	Dam	Res	Hits
Humanoid	3	55	5	2	32	4	2	8

Flying, Poison Strike, Strike, Night Vision, Vision 2, Poison Protection, Charge

Big Beetle

Type	Lvl	Cost	At	Def	Mov	Dam	Res	Hits
Creature	3	120	5	3	40	4	4	13

Walking, Cave Crawling, Poison Strike, Strike, Tunneling, Poison Protection, Wall Crushing

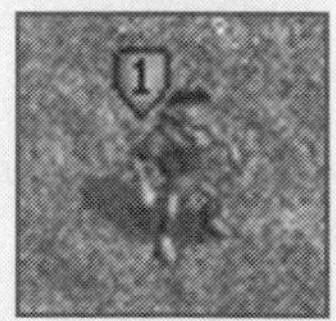

Troll

Type	Lvl	Cost	At	Def	Mov	Dam	Res	Hits
Creature	3	75	6	3	28	7	4	12

Walking, Strike, Night Vision, Regeneration

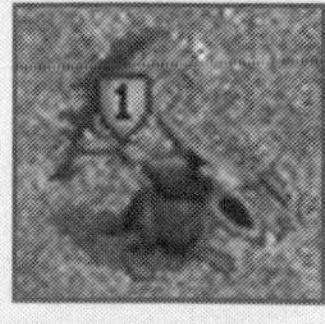

Karagh

Type	Lvl	Cost	At	Def	Mov	Dam	Res	Hits
Creature	4	195	7	4	44	8	7	21

Walking, Cave Crawling, Strike, Night Vision, Cause Fear, Fearless, Poison Protection, Charge

Orcs

Kobold

Type	Lvl	Cost	At	Def	Mov	Dam	Res	Hits
Humanoid	1	15	4	2	24	2	3	4

Walking, Cave Crawling, Poison Immunity, Poison Strike, Strike, Night Vision

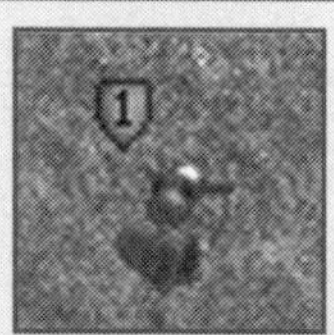

Archer

Type	Lvl	Cost	At	Def	Mov	Dam	Res	Hits
Humanoid	1	15	3	2	26	2	3	5

Walking, Archery

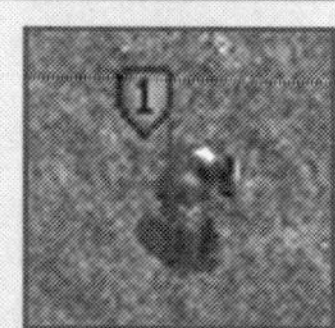

Swordsman

Type	Lvl	Cost	At	Def	Mov	Dam	Res	Hits
Humanoid	1	17	4	2	26	4	3	5

Walking, Strike

Battering Ram

Type	Lvl	Cost	At	Def	Mov	Dam	Res	Hits
Machine	1	23	1	2	20	1	3	10

Walking, Poison Immunity, Fearless, Cold Protection, Wall Crushing

Shaman

Type	Lvl	Cost	At	Def	Mov	Dam	Res	Hits
Humanoid	2	30	3	2	26	2	4	5

Walking, Magic Strike, Strike, Turn Undead 1, Night Vision, Healing, Dispel Magic 1, Magic Bolts

Heavy Cavalry

Type	Lvl	Cost	At	Def	Mov	Dam	Res	Hits
Humanoid	2	39	5	3	32	4	3	8

Walking, Strike, Charge

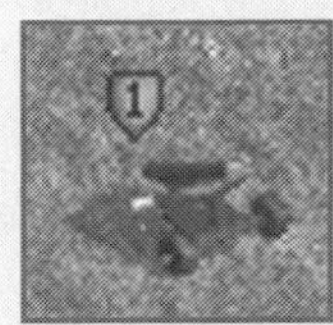

Shredder Bolt

Type	Lvl	Cost	At	Def	Mov	Dam	Res	Hits
Machine	2	75	1	2	20	1	3	7

Walking, Poison Immunity, Shoot Black Javelin, Fearless, Cold Protection

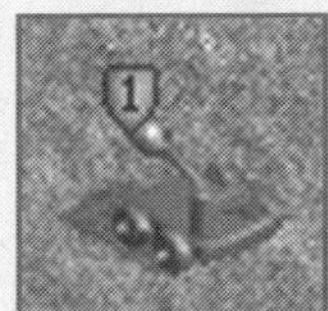

Catapult

Type	Lvl	Cost	At	Def	Mov	Dam	Res	Hits
Machine	2	58	1	2	20	1	3	8

Walking, Poison Immunity, Hurl Boulder, Fearless, Cold Protection

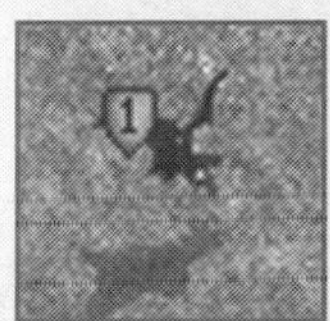

Doom Bat

Type	Lvl	Cost	At	Def	Mov	Dam	Res	Hits
Creature	3	55	4	3	28	4	3	7

Flying, Poison Strike, Strike, Night Vision, Cause Fear, Poison Protection, Underground Concealment

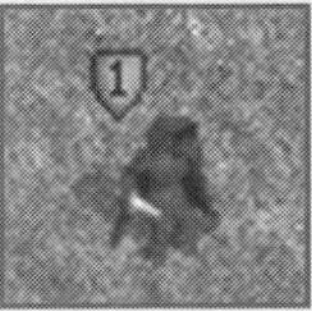

Assassin

Type	Lvl	Cost	At	Def	Mov	Dam	Res	Hits
Humanoid	3	75	5	3	28	3	3	7

Walking, Poison Strike, Strike, Marksmanship 1, Wall Climbing, Poison Darts, Concealment

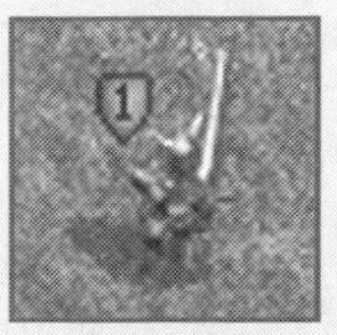

Warlord

Type	Lvl	Cost	At	Def	Mov	Dam	Res	Hits
Humanoid	3	105	7	6	26	6	5	14

Walking, Strike, Round Attack

Red Dragon

Type	Lvl	Cost	At	Def	Mov	Dam	Res	Hits
Creature	4	235	6	7	32	5	8	18

Flying, Fire Immunity, Strike, Dragon, Vision 2, Fearless, Fire Breath

Player's Manual

Undead

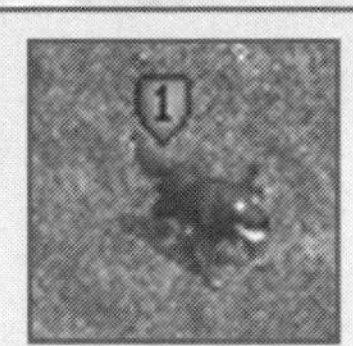

Hell Hound

Type	Lvl	Cost	At	Def	Mov	Dam	Res	Hits
Creature	1	20	4	3	32	2	3	5

Walking, Fire Strike, Strike, Regeneration, Fearless, Death Protection, Fire Protection

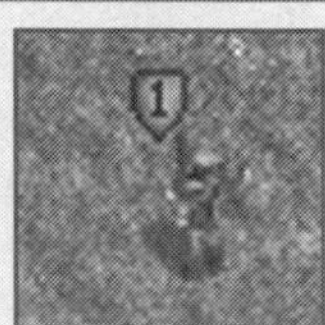

Swordsman

Type	Lvl	Cost	At	Def	Mov	Dam	Res	Hits
Humanoid	1	18	4	2	26	3	3	5

Walking, Poison Immunity, Strike, Regeneration, Fearless, Fire Protection, Lightning Protection, Cold Protection

Bone Ram

Type	Lvl	Cost	At	Def	Mov	Dam	Res	Hits
Machine	1	25	2	2	20	1	3	10

Walking, Poison Immunity, Regeneration, Fearless, Fire Protection, Lightning Protection, Cold Protection, Wall Crushing

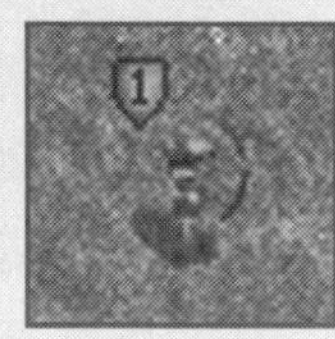

Archer

Type	Lvl	Cost	At	Def	Mov	Dam	Res	Hits
Humanoid	1	18	4	2	26	1	3	5

Walking, Poison Immunity, Death Immunity, Archery, Regeneration, Fearless, Fire Protection, Lightning Protection, Cold Protection

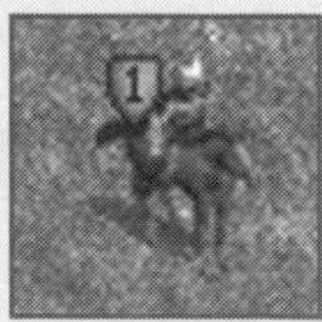

Knight

Type	Lvl	Cost	At	Def	Mov	Dam	Res	Hits
Humanoid	2	40	5	3	36	3	3	7

Walking, Poison Immunity, Death Immunity, Strike, Regeneration, Fearless, Fire Protection, Lightning Protection, Cold Protection, Charge

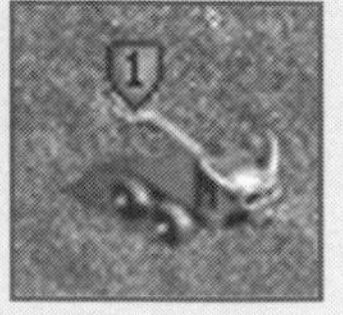

Skull Thrower

Type	Lvl	Cost	At	Def	Mov	Dam	Res	Hits
Machine	2	60	1	2	60	1	3	7

Walking, Poison Immunity, Hurl Boulder, Regeneration, Fearless, Fire Protection, Lightning Protection, Cold Protection

Doom Priest

Type	Lvl	Cost	At	Def	Mov	Dam	Res	Hits
Humanoid	2	42	3	2	26	2	4	5

Walking, Poison Immunity, Death Immunity, Death Strike, Strike, Dominate, Regeneration, Dispel Magic 1, Fearless, Fire Protection, Lightning Protection, Cold Protection, Black Bolts

Ballista

Type	Lvl	Cost	At	Def	Mov	Dam	Res	Hits
Machine	2	56	3	4	20	1	3	7

Walking, Poison Immunity, Shoot Javelin, Fearless, Cold Protection

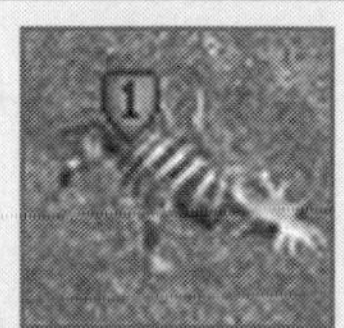

Bone Horror

Type	Lvl	Cost	At	Def	Mov	Dam	Res	Hits
Creature	3	104	5	3	26	5	4	19

Walking, Poison Immunity, Death Immunity, Death Strike, Strike, Regeneration, Fearless, Fire Protection, Lightning Protection, Cold Protection, Wall Crushing

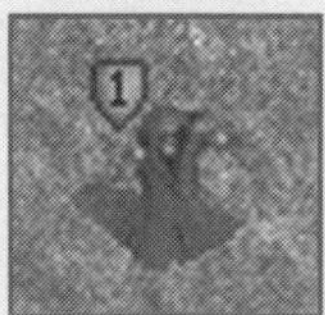

Wraith

Type	Lvl	Cost	At	Def	Mov	Dam	Res	Hits
Creature	3	75	4	2	26	3	4	6

Walking, Fire Immunity, Cold Immunity, Poison Immunity, Death Immunity, Physical Immunity, Death Strike, Strike, Regeneration, Fearless, Pass Wall, Lightning Protection, Life Stealing

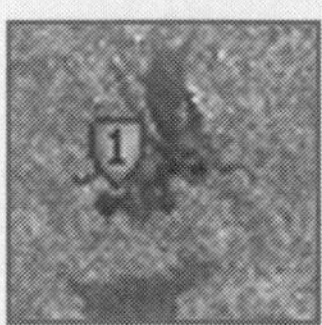

Demon

Type	Lvl	Cost	At	Def	Mov	Dam	Res	Hits
Creature	3	105	7	4	30	6	4	10

Flying, Fire Immunity, Poison Immunity, Death Immunity, Poison Strike, Strike, Regeneration, Vision 2, Fearless

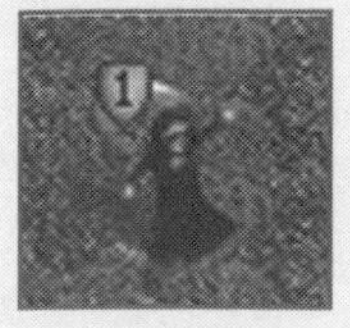

Undead Reaper

Type	Lvl	Cost	At	Def	Mov	Dam	Res	Hits
Creature	4	210	7	4	26	5	10	15

Walking, Poison Immunity, Death Immunity, Death Strike, Strike, Regeneration, Invoke Death, Cause Fear, Fearless, Path of Decay, Lightning Protection, Cold Protection

Appendix 1 - Spell Descriptions

Life Level 1

Bless

Type	Casting Cost
Unit Enchantment	10

This spell bestows a single unit with a blessing from heaven. It obtains a +1 bonus to defense and resistance, as well as a limited resistance to Death magic.

Remedy

Type	Casting Cost
Unit Enchantment	8

This spell heals a unit by 5 hit points, as well as removing any non-magical handicaps from that unit.

Rejuvenate

Type	Casting Cost
Global	5

This spell changes a small area of the global map from desert, steppe, icelands, and wasteland to fertile grasslands.

Solar Flare

Type	Casting Cost
Combat	6

Projects a blast of Holy fire at a target.

Attack: 6
Damage: 4
Holy Damage

Life Level 2

Holy Champion

Type	Casting Cost
Unit Enchantment	25

Gives a bonus of +2 to attack and defense against evil units.

Holy Woods

Type	Casting Cost
Global	20

A barrier of trees imbued with holy power will rise up when this spell is cast. All units of evil alignment will be subject to holy damage while passing through.

Turn Undead

Type	Casting Cost
Combat	11

During Combat, this spell can be used to damage any undead enemies you face. It has no effect on any other type of unit.

Attack: 7
Damage: 7

Recall Spirits

Type	Casting Cost
Combat	28

Resurrects dead units during combat to fight on your side. They will appear in the form of Spirit Puppets instead of their normal selves.

Life Level 3

High Prayer

Type	Casting Cost
Combat	36

When cast during combat, the forces of good will converge on the battlefield, giving all units friendly to the caster +1 bonuses to Defense, Attack, Resistance, and Damage.

Sacred Wrath

Type	Casting Cost
Combat	32

This spell calls the fury of the gods to the battlefield, resulting in a powerful burst of holy energy that damages all units, be they friend or foe.

Attack: 5
Damage: 5
Holy Damage

Resurrect Hero

Type	Casting Cost
Global	66

This magic can resurrect a Hero that has died previously during the game. As death is a traumatic experience however, the Hero will need some persuasion (in the form of gold) and a compatible race and alignment to take up the cause again.

Tranquility

Type	Casting Cost
World Enchantment	60

A sense of harmony envelopes the land when this spell is cast, causing race relationships to steadily improve and unrest in cities to decrease.

Life Level 4

Crusade

Type	Casting Cost
World Enchantment	280

This powerful spell causes the independent forces of Light to organize attacks against the evil races of the land. This spell only lasts three turns.

Divine Storm

Type	Casting Cost
Global	105

This creates a powerful storm of holy energy that affects a large area of the Global map, damaging all units within the storm and transforming the land into fertile grasslands.

Life Mastery

Type	Casting Cost
World Enchantment	360

When cast, all enemy evil units must successfully resist or feel the effects of a Fear spell. Also, all friendly units are considered Blessed and all Death sphere spells cost double while this enchantment is in effect. A Gold Dragon will appear at each Life Node, under the control of the player who owns the Node.

Summon Gold Dragon

Type	Casting Cost
Summons	210

This summons a huge, divine Dragon capable of flight and possessing a powerful Divine Breath attack, as well as many special abilities.

Death Level 1

Dark Gift

Type	Casting Cost
Unit Enchantment	10

Gives a single unit Death Strike, which enables it to deal Death Damage during combat, and +1 to damage.

Summon Black Spider

Type	Casting Cost
Summons	31

Summons a giant Black Spider to fight for the caster.

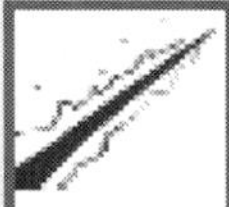

Death Ray

Type	Casting Cost
Combat	4

Death Ray directs a bolt of unholy energy toward an enemy unit during combat.

Attack: 6
Damage: 4
Death Damage

Disease Cloud

Type	Casting Cost
Combat	9

This combat spell will cause a small cloud of disease-ridden magical energy to appear on the battlefield, sickening units inside it.

Attack: 5
Damage: 3
Death Damage

Death Level 2

Evil Champion

Type	Casting Cost
Unit Enchantment	25

When cast on a unit, that unit becomes a powerful champion of the Death sphere, giving it +2 bonuses to attack and defense against units of Good alignment.

Evil Woods

Type	Casting Cost
Global	20

When cast, a magical barrier of haunted woods will spring from the ground. All good units attempting to pass through will be subject to Death damage.

Animate Dead

Type	Casting Cost
Combat	28

This spell, when cast after units have perished during battle, will reanimate their corpses into Skeleton Warriors under the caster's control. These Skeletons will only remain for the duration of the battle, after which they disappear.

Terror

Type	Casting Cost
Combat	15

When cast during battle, all units that fail to resist will have their morale substantially lowered. This can sometimes result in paralyzation.

Attack: 5

Morale Penalty: -3

Death Level 3

Animate Ruins

Type	Casting Cost
City Enchantment	42

If a city has been razed or looted, this spell will rebuild the ruins as a new town with the caster's race, and resurrect the population as skeleton warriors.

Pestilence

Type	Casting Cost
Global	55

This spell creates a large cloud of poison that floats across the global map, moving a random direction each turn. All units in the cloud will suffer poison damage.

Mind Decay

Type	Casting Cost
Combat	28

This spell will summon the forces of darkness to attack the mind of a single enemy unit during combat, causing it damage every turn. Has no effect on Undead units.

Attack: 6
Damage: 5

Animate Hero

Type	Casting Cost
Global	66

Use this spell to animate a deceased Hero. The Hero's alignment and race must be compatible with your own, or he may decide not to join you. A small amount of gold will also be required to convince the Hero to become a soldier again.

Death Level 4

Death Mastery

Type	Casting Cost
World Enchantment	360

While this spell is in effect, the unexplored area will expand 1 hex per turn for all players. All good units are also Cursed, unless they manage to successfully resist (attack: 6). Life spells cost double. A Black Dragon will appear at each Death Node, under the control of the player who owns the Node.

Death Storm

Type	Casting Cost
Global	105

When cast on the Global map, the spellcaster can direct a powerful blast of negative energy towards a large area, turning it to corrupted wastelands and inflicting large amounts of Death damage on all units within the area of effect.

Hatred

Type	Casting Cost
World Enchantment	110

This spell causes relations between all races to deteriorate, fracturing alliances and increasing the chances of hostilities with neutral parties.

Summon Black Dragon

Type	Casting Cost
Summons	210

This spell summons an evil Black Dragon to serve in the caster's army. These powerful creatures are capable of destroying most units outright with their powerful breath attack, as well as possessing a host of special abilities.

Air Level 1

Haste

Type	Casting Cost
Unit Enchantment	10

This adds 10 to any one unit's number of movement points. Useful for catapults and other slow-moving units.

Bird's View

Type	Casting Cost
Global	8

Bird's View reveals a large area of the map around the caster. Be advised that it does not work underground.

Vaporize

Type	Casting Cost
Combat	4

Attempts to vaporize target's outer body.

Attack: 5
Damage: 5
Physical Damage

Chain Lightning

Type	Casting Cost
Combat	8

The combat spell Chain Lightning strikes a single unit with a lightning attack and then jumps to other enemy units nearby, damaging them as well.

Attack: 5
Damage: 4
Lightning Damage

Air Level 2

Winds of Fury

Type	Casting Cost
Combat	12

During combat, attacks one unit with powerful winds, blowing them away from their location and damaging flying units.

Attack: 7
Damage: 5
Physical Damage

Great Eagle

Type	Casting Cost
Summons	38

Summons a far-seeing Eagle to join the caster. These make superb scouts due to their excellent vision.

Freeze Water

Type	Casting Cost
Global	28

This spell allows the caster to freeze the water of a river or ocean, preventing passage of ships and allowing land units to walk across.

Cold Breath

Type	Casting Cost
Combat	22

During battle, this spell will freeze the target with a blast of frozen air.

Attack: 5
Damage: 5
Cold Damage

Air Level 3

Call Hero

Type	Casting Cost
Global	52

This will call a Hero to join the caster. A fee and compatible alignment are still required, or else the Hero may decide not to join you and instead remain non-aligned. This is not a summon spell, and does not drain any mana after the spell is completed.

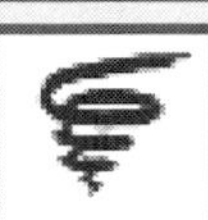

Tornado

Type	Casting Cost
Global	56

Invokes a magical vortex over the target party, hurling some or all members far away. Is most effective against low-level units positioned in plains.

Shockwave

Type	Casting Cost
Combat	22

Blasts the area around the caster with powerful waves of sonic energy. Only affects the immediate vicinity around the spell caster in combat.

Wind Walking

Type	Casting Cost
Unit Enchantment	44

This spell will give any unit the ability to fly.

Air Level 4

Air Mastery

Type	Casting Cost
World Enchantment	360

Once cast, this spell will make the winds favor the caster's side, resulting in double movement speeds for all ships and fliers. All enemy ships and fliers will have their movement speed cut in half, and all Earth spells will cost double. An Air Elemental will appear at each Air Node, under the control of the player who owns the Node.

Air Elemental

Type	Casting Cost
Summons	194

Summons a powerful, flying Air Elemental.

Watcher

Type	Casting Cost
Global	110

Summons a magical entity that watches over a large area. Watchers can see concealed or invisible enemies.

Lightning Storm

Type	Casting Cost
Global	80

This spell summons a lightning strike over a small area of the global map. All units and structures within the area of effect are subject to Lightning damage.

Earth Level 1

Stone Skin

Type	Casting Cost
Unit Enchantment	10

This spell hardens a unit's skin, increasing its defense (+2 bonus) from physical attacks.

Great Boar

Type	Casting Cost
Summons	25

This summons a wild boar to fight on the caster's side.

Entangle

Type	Casting Cost
Combat	6

Attempts to entangle target with tentacles from beneath for the duration of the battle.

Attack: 7

Slow

Type	Casting Cost
Combat	*3*

Attempts to cut the target's movement points in half for the duration of battle.

Attack: 7

Earth Level 2

Free Movement

Type	Casting Cost
Unit Enchantment	12

Units with this spell will find their footing much easier than those without, resulting in easier movement across forests and mountains.

Gold Rush

Type	Casting Cost
City Enchantment	40

This spell doubles the gold income of any town it is cast upon.

Poison Woods

Type	Casting Cost
Global	32

This spell sprouts poisonous bushes that will damage all units that attempt to pass through them.

Stoning

Type	Casting Cost
Combat	12

This spell will send 8 stones towards a target during combat, each with a separate chance to hit and do damage.

Attack: 4
Damage: 2
Physical Damage

Earth Level 3

Concealment

Type	Casting Cost
Unit Enchantment	36

This spell will hide the enchanted unit from the view of the enemy. It will only be visible to the opponent when adjacent to one of his or her units.

Enchant Roads

Type	Casting Cost
World Enchantment	80

After this spell is cast, all troop movement cost is reduced by one third when travelling by foot on a road.

Level Terrain

Type	Casting Cost
Global	52

This powerful magic will reduce mountains and hills to level ground, allowing ground-based units to pass easily

Tremors

Type	Casting Cost
Combat	38

This combat spell will cause the ground to shake violently, causing massive damage to all structures and units.

Attack: 5
Damage: 5
Physical Damage

Earth Level 4

Earth Mastery

Type	Casting Cost
World Enchantment	200

This spell not only causes all Air spells to cost double, but imbues all friendly units with a Stone Skin spell at the beginning of every turn. An Earth Elemental will appear at each Earth Node, under the control of the player who owns the Node.

Earth Elemental

Type	Casting Cost
Summons	196

When a magician casts this spell, a powerful Earth Elemental is summoned. Though slow, it has the ability to crush walls and tunnel through earth, as well as being destructively powerful in combat.

Raise Terrain

Type	Casting Cost
Global	80

Acting as the opposite of the spell Level Terrain, Raise Terrain will instead cause the terrain to rise into mountains, allowing the caster to block off areas of the map.

Town Quake

Type	Casting Cost
City Enchantment	95

When cast on an enemy town, a powerful earthquake will tear through the target, causing massive damage to the city's buildings, walls, and all units inside.

Fire Level 1

Fury

Type	Casting Cost
Unit Enchantment	7

Target unit is imbued with a destructive fury, giving it a +2 bonus to attack, but the blinding rage results in a –1 defensive penalty.

Fire Sprite

Type	Casting Cost
Summons	28

Summons a minor creature from the Fire plane to fight for the caster's cause.

Flame Arrow

Type	Casting Cost
Combat	4

This sends a bolt of fire towards an enemy unit in combat.

Attack: 5
Damage: 5
Physical Damage
Fire Damage

Call Flames

Type	Casting Cost
Combat	6

All units present take damage and flammable materials are ignited.

Attack: 7
Damage: 3
Fire Damage

Fire Level 2

Fire Halo

Type	Casting Cost
Unit Enchantment	15

The target unit becomes linked to the Fire plane, giving it fire immunity and the ability to ignite flammable materials on contact.

Cloud of Ashes

Type	Casting Cost
Global	27

When cast on the global map, a small, obscuring cloud of dust will appear, hiding all units within the cloud from view of the enemy. Be warned, though, that although the enemy will not be able to see your units in the Cloud, neither will you be able to see theirs.

Fire Breath

Type	Casting Cost
Combat	18

When used in combat, a cone of Fire will severely damage a target a short range from the caster.

Attack: 5
Damage: 5
Fire Damage

Swarm

Type	Casting Cost
Combat	16

A group of fireflies attacks the target unit, and any nearby beings, without descrimination.

Attack: 5
Damage: 1
Fire Damage

Fire Level 3

Anarchy

Type	Casting Cost
City Enchantment	48

When cast upon a city on the Global map, the city's inhabitants are enraged and begin to rebel. A strong garrison is required to keep the city from full rebellion. This spell does not affect neutral towns.

Fire Barrier

Type	Casting Cost
Global	45

Creates a large barrier of magical flame across a swath of the Global map. All units attempting to pass through the flames are subjected to Fire damage

Fireball

Type	Casting Cost
Combat	20

During Combat, this spell creates a powerful burst of Fire energy. It will explode upon impact, igniting flammable material within the area of effect and damaging walls.

Attack: 7
Damage: 6
Fire Damage
Wall Damage

Sacrificial Flame

Type	Casting Cost
Combat	22

The caster channels energy from the Fire plane through his body, causing him minute damage while causing severe damage to a target area.

Fire Level 4

Fire Mastery

Type	Casting Cost
World Enchantment	200

This spell causes the forces of Fire to sear the minds of all. Unaligned troops will become enraged and attack their neighbors. All Water spells cost double. A Fire Elemental will appear at each Fire Node, under the control of the player who owns the Node.

Fire Elemental

Type	Casting Cost
Summons	185

Summons a poweful Fire Elemental which is devastating in combat. The mere touch of this creature is capable of setting units on fire, and it can also wield the Call Flames spell at will during battle.

Warmonger

Type	Casting Cost
City Enchantment	110

When cast upon a city, all units subsequently built there will start at the Veteran experience level.

Fire Storm

Type	Casting Cost
Global	105

Calls upon the forces of fire to explode in a large area on the Global map. All units in the area will take Fire damage, and wildfires will burn, even after the storm is finished.

Water Level 1

Summon Frog

Type	Casting Cost
Summons	25

This spell will summon a large, amphibious frog to fight for you.

Healing Water

Type	Casting Cost
Unit Enchantment	20

This unit spell will heal a single unit to maximum hit points instantly..

Ice Shards

Type	Casting Cost
Combat	8

During combat, you can use this spell to shred your enemy with sharp ice pellets over long distances.

Attack: 4
Damage: 4
Physical Damage

Ooze

Type	Casting Cost
Combat	6

This spell creates a large area of mud during combat. Ground-based units attempting to pass over the sticky terrain will find their movement hindered, resulting in their speed being halved.

Water Level 2

Water Walking

Type	Casting Cost
Unit Enchantment	14

This gives any land-based unit the ability to walk across bodies of water..

Vortex

Type	Casting Cost
Global	25

When cast on the global map, a massive whirlpool will form on a single water hex, dealing serious damage to all water-based units there.

Geyser

Type	Casting Cost
Combat	12

This combat spell lifts the target up in a large burst of water, then drops it from a great height, dealing serious damage.

Attack: 5
Damage: 5
Physical Damage

Frost Beam

Type	Casting Cost
Combat	14

Icy water pours down, attempting to freeze units in the target area in a block of ice.

Attack: 8
Damage: 3
Cold Damage

Water Level 3

Liquid Form

Type	Casting Cost
Unit Enchantment	30

Binds a unit to the Water plane, allowing it to swim, and reducing damage from physical attacks.

Great Hail

Type	Casting Cost
Combat	32

During Combat, this spell will bring down a storm of hail over a small area of the map, damaging all units therein.

Attack: 5
Damage: 5
Physical Damage

Healing Showers

Type	Casting Cost
Global	24

When cast on an area of the Global map, this spell restores the health of both the units and the land there, due to the restoring effects of the amazingly pure water.

Fountain of Life

Type	Casting Cost
City Enchantment	80

This spell transforms a city into a healing center, healing all units that enter the town to full health at the end of every turn.

Water Level 4

Water Mastery

Type	Casting Cost
World Enchantment	360

When cast, all fire spells cost double, and thick mist obscures the sight of the spellcaster's opponents, halving vision for all enemies. A Water Elemental will appear at each Water Node, under the control of the player who owns the Node.

Flood

Type	Casting Cost
World Enchantment	380

This powerful spell causes the rivers and oceans of the world to grow in size, resulting in flooding all across the map. While the floods won't penetrate city walls, all stacks of units that are on a section of the map when it becomes flooded will drown.

Water Elemental

Type	Casting Cost
Summons	185

Summons a creature from the Water plane. The Water Elemental can swim and, due to it's liquid body, is immune to damage due to physical weapons.

Ice Storm

Type	Casting Cost
Global	105

This spell covers a large area with ice and freezes water solid. All units caught within the storm are subject to Cold damage.

Cosmos Level 1

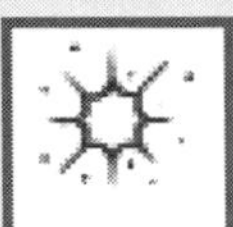

Enchant Weapon

Type	Casting Cost
Unit Enchantment	10

This spell enchants a unit's weapon, making it magical and giving it +1 bonuses to both Attack and Damage..

Dispel Magic

Type	Casting Cost
Global	5

If your unit has become the target of a negative enchantment, use this spell to attempt to remove it.

Cosmos Level 2

Disjunction

Type	Casting Cost
Global	25

Using this spell, you can attempt to remove an opponent's global enchantment.

Warp Party

Type	Casting Cost
Global	20

This spell will warp the caster's party to a random location nearby. It's range is limited, but it is a fast method of escape or exploration. It can also teleport the party underground at random.

Cosmos Level 3

Anti-Magic Shell

Type	Casting Cost
City Enchantment	76

This spell creates a powerful barrier of anti-magic energy above a city, nullifying the effects of spells that are cast in (or upon) the city.

Town Gate

Type	Casting Cost
Global	52

A spellcaster wielding this spell can teleport himself and his party to any other town under the Leader's control, from anywhere on the map.

Cosmos Level 4

Power Leak

Type	Casting Cost
World Enchantment	110

This spell cuts the magic power of all players in half.

Spell Ward

Type	Casting Cost
World Enchantment	130

Creates a barrier limiting the use of World Enchantments. No player may cast or disjunct a World Enchantment until Spell Ward is removed (or disjuncted).

Appendix 2

The History of the Valley of Wonders

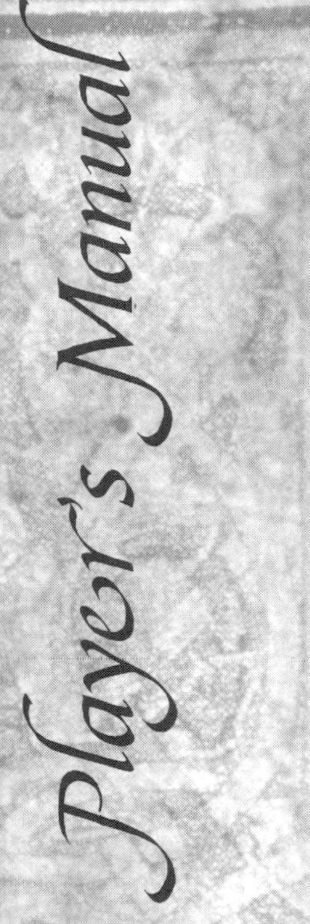

0 LIR: (Lord Inioch's Reign) - Inioch is crowned Emperor of the Elven Kingdom and his father retires to Evermor. He is the undisputed supreme monarch over the Blessed Continent. From the Verdant Court in the Valley of Wonders, Inioch's will is law.

800 LIR: A new race called the High Men appear before the Verdant Court. Inioch hides the official communications between the Verdant Court and the High Men, keeping their requests to himself. Instead, Inioch forms a political coalition among all the races of reason to promote peace with the new comers, assigning many scholars to lead the effort. They are called the Keepers. The Keepers, grossly ill-informed of High Men intentions, satiate the strange newcomers with their intentions of peace.

801 LIR: The High Men leave to work in their 'garden.'

870 LIR: Inioch announces his wife's pregnancy. The Verdant Kingdom rejoices for the duration of the pregnancy.

878 LIR: After 8 years of pregnancy, Inioch's wife gives birth to Meandor, but the celebrations are cut short. Inioch's first wife, Julia, dies in childbirth. Her body is taken to Evermor. The celebration of the new heir's birth is overshadowed by the obligation to mourn the loss of the Elven Queen.

898 LIR: The minimal period of mourning expires, and Inioch marries Elwyn the following day. Meandor, still only a child, resents Elwyn and finds the haste of their marriage an insult to his mother.

961 LIR: Inioch announces that Queen Elwyn is pregnant. Inioch justifies the new child's conception by claiming the child will replace his first wife among the Elven population. Factions led by Meandor in the Verdant Court refuse to celebrate the child's coming.

962 LIR: Vessels appear on the horizon, and some island nations issue complaints about the migration of an uncouth race called Humans. After overwhelming many of these islands, the first Human explorers continue on to the Blessed Continent, following after retreating ships.

965 LIR: The first Humans reach the Valley of Wonders and form a small colony. The Keepers insist they be allowed to come and instruct the Dwarven Sentinels to open the Valley passageways to all.

966 LIR: The Human colonies experience hardships and the Verdant Court remains reluctant to show aid. Rumors abound among the Court that perhaps some of the cause of this hardship is Court induced. The Humans turn to more dangerous allies, seeking help from the oppression of their kind.

969 LIR: Queen Elwyn gives birth to a baby girl. Other races clamor about the influx of Human population, as comfort and ease of life become scarcer. Inioch's political enemies view the new child as evidence that there will soon be no room for both the growing Elven population and the ever-burgeoning humanity. The Keepers back Inioch, who claims that the fact that the child is female is proof that she was meant to replace his dead wife. To acknowledge that replacement, he names the child Julia—the name of his first wife (and Meandor's mother). Meandor is less than pleased. Celebrations honoring Julia end abruptly with the news that Human factions have discovered evidence suggesting that factions within Verdant Court have funded and organized the plagues and persecution against Human colonies.

970 LIR: FALL OF INIOCH'S COURT: The Humans declare war upon the Northern Kingdom, and together with their allies, they strike against many of the Kingdom's most precious holdings, including Inioch's Court. Meandor allies with a secret faction of Elven rebels known as Dark Elves. After a twisted scheme of political intrigue, the Verdant Court falls to a force of Humans. Inioch is slain. The palace is razed. Clutching her newborn child in her arms, Queen Elwyn flees the Verdant Court with the help of the Keepers. Meandor is gravely wounded and mistaken for dead. The slaughter is so great that the Humans pile the bodies in the ruined central court and refuse to settle near it, leaving the center to stink in the wind. Not understanding Elven physiology, Meandor's gravely- wounded body is thrown into the heap of dead to rot. After many weeks, with the aid of an unknown force, he escapes the press of the dead and joins with the Dark Elves. The Keepers manage to hold the Humans back temporarily and establish a non-aggression pact.

971 LIR: The Humans claim the Valley of Wonders as their own. Any race refusing to accept Human sovereignty is to be driven from the Valley. The Keepers negotiate a brief time for migration. Queen Elwyn gathers the Elves, pleading with them to leave the Valley and go elsewhere, but many stubbornly refuse. Many Elves want to stay and fight, desiring vengeance and demanding that she lead them in the struggle to reclaim the Valley. After many debates, she takes Julia and leaves.

973 LIR: Tired of Keeper efforts to stall the evacuation of Elven settlements from the Valley of Wonders, the Humans turn to their swords to force the migration of all others therein. The Elves are scattered, fleeing in every direction, as they become the primary targets of Human aggression. The Dwarves, at great expense, try to close the mountain passes to the Humans, allowing the Elves time to escape. Only a few Human armies make it through to pursue the fleeing Elves. From the Pass of Grief, a mass of Humans overwhelm the Elves, chasing them to the Toll Rock Wood. The Humans trap the desperate fleeing Elves and all that cannot escape via boats are slaughtered.

974 LIR: Silvanus is founded as a bastion of Elf power. Unlike Queen Elwyn, they refuse to retreat further at the press of Humans. They raise an army and destroy any Humans responsible for the slaughter of Toll Rock Wood, and drive all Humans back to the Valley of Wonders. In the coming centuries, only the Elves of Silvanus consistently succeed in resisting Human expansion.

975 LIR: The Dwarven Sentinels break and fall back to settlements nearby. The Humans begin building massive fortresses and continue to hold the Valley, as more Humans arrive by sea.

977 LIR: The Dark Elves crown Meandor the rightful monarch, in Inioch's place, over the Valley of Wonders. Few races acknowledge the act, and a majority of races back Queen Elwyn, while others simply refuse to accept any ruler.

983 LIR: The Dwarves, wearied by a decade of holding the Humans within the boundaries of the Valley of Storms, begin to see their efforts are in vain. With little support from the other races, they are forced to consider their own survival. They decide to expand their underground cities, centering upon Deepmir. They begin massive feats of construction and excavation.

985 LIR: After a short period of being ignored, Meandor forms the Cult of Storms, dedicated to the destruction of humanity. The Cult adopts tactics similar to the Keepers', but with the intent of destruction, rather than preserving peace and serenity. Meandor attempts to flatter the Elves of Silvanus into joining with him, but the Elves refuse to have any part of his plots, and Meandor's plans for retaking the Valley are largely ignored.

987 LIR: Human strongholds within the Valley of Wonders are so established and impregnable that the Humans increase their colonization into the Valley at an unprecedented speed. Fleet upon fleet of travelers arrive. The Valley continues to fill with Humans, and they eye the surrounding lands with hunger. The Cult tries to excite the nations to action against the Humans, citing their rapid expansion as the doom of all others. But too many races have been beaten by previous engagements against the Humans to really do much more than nod and sigh.

989 LIR: After repeated defeats at the hands of the Humans, the Cult of Storms suffers numerous desertions and many bloody outbreaks of civil strife. The Cult eventually gains control over most of the evil races, but not without suffering many setbacks and losing many of its more powerful Leaders to sedition and rebellion.

993 LIR: The Cult's attacks of terror against the Humans result in Humans attacking the fair Elves, mistaking them for their attackers. Keeper negotiations with Humans crumble as a result, for Humans do not believe the Keepers and Cult to be separate organizations. To prove to the Humans that they are different, the Keepers realize they can no longer ignore the actions of the Cult. In the Keepers war against the Cult, Elf and Dark Elf clash in a terrible conflict.

994 LIR: Humans begin to conquer the lands surrounding the Valley of Wonders. Each race braces for inexorable Human expansion, while eyeing each other's holdings with the hope of gaining some advantage.

999 LIR: The Halflings donate the Isle of Aldor to the Elves and draw most of their people into the United Cities. After nearly thirty years of wandering and fleeing, Queen Elwyn and her refugees found a new court. She is proclaimed rightful ruler over the Elves. The Elves of Aldor accept her as ruler, and the Halflings back her appointment with unprecedented enthusiasm.

1000 LIR: REIGN of CHAOS. A number of key alliances crumble. The Keepers' only shelter is found within Elwyn's court and among the Halflings. The races divide and gather to themselves, seeking to exert as much influence as possible. Many of the evil races view the disintegration of harmony upon the surface as an opportunity to attack.

Meandor claims that he should be the rightful heir supreme, as by Elven custom the rightful heir is traditionally named in the 1000th year of a king's rule. Yet it is unprecedented that an Elven King die before the end of his rule (as Inioch has), and most Elves fear Meandor—even those few who follow him fear the outward changes in his appearance and the company he keeps. Following Elven tradition, he would have to marry Elwyn, and Elwyn will have nothing to do with him. Many Elves look to Julia as a true heir to the Northern Throne.

Meandor declares that, due to their reluctance to crown him, the fair surface Elves have committed high treason and vows to see them all punished. This, of course, does not win many converts to his side. And still, the threat of Human expansion increases.

1001 LIR: With the Elves weakened and the order of protection crumbled, Orcs pour from their caves, seeing the latest chaos as an opportunity for easy plunder and a chance to establish themselves as 'chief bullies' in a world of weaklings.

1020 LIR: After the official period of mourning ends, Meandor strikes against his former subjects, the fair Elves. He begins a reign of terror and vows to destroy all those who will not join him in his quest to rule the Valley and destroy humanity. Heartwood Forest is badly scarred by a most terrible skirmish.

1023 LIR: After many losses and migrations, the Dwarves are more numerous in Deepmir than in any other place on the land.

1025 LIR: Julia joins the Keepers, and begins her training among them. She is celebrated as the youngest Elf to join their order. She is sharp, and beautiful. All who behold her view her as the one true heiress to Inioch's reign. Meandor's many attempts to assassinate her fail.

1048 LIR: After the most severe winter ever recorded, the Humans make a new enemy: The Frostlings.

1080 LIR: The Azrac Empire pushes against the influx of new races into its territory. Under the guise of a Ritual War of Racial Purification'. refugee races find themselves trapped between a mass of Human invaders and the sacrosanct empire of the Azracs.

1082 LIR: After purifying their boundaries, the Azracs turn their attention to capturing key treasures in the North and begin a great campaign to take control of the Blessed Continent.

1084 LIR: Azracs fight for control of the Canal.

1087 LIR: The Humans expand their influence, pushing the Azracs from the southern and eastern sides of the Valley. After a great battle, they capture the Ashen Steppe.

1090 LIR: The Azracs, Lizardmen, Humans, and Orcs clash in a bloody contest over Barondir Bay.

1096 LIR: Seeing that individual racial forces are insufficient to hold back the waves of Humans and Azracs, the Keepers use the opportunity to forge powerful alliances against both, and manage to organize a strike force against the invaders.

1098 LIR: The Keeper Alliance manages to push the Azracs from the richest portions of the Northern Kingdom. The Azracs, who know defeat is imminent, steal the Trump of the Dead and threaten to blow it, should aggressors seek vengeance, or attempt to take advantage of their weakened state and capture their ancient holdings.

1101 LIR: 'Someone' blows the trump. Azracs deny that they did the deed.

1102 LIR: The Undead sweep over the lands.

1111 LIR: Halflings and Goblins fight over an obscure area of mountain lands. All races of the Northern Kingdom prepare for the waves of death, which are surging toward even the most peaceful lands.

1115 LIR: The Dark Elves refuse to join the alliance against the Undead. Though generally silent during the invasion, which occurs mostly on the sunlit surface, they do manage to take a few surface possessions, including a fertile area near Durlag.

1122 LIR: Many Humans are seduced by the power of the Undead. Death cults and necromancers run rampant, spreading the false doctrines of death. The fair races of the world suffer greatly.

1127 LIR: Races crowd into the largest walled cities at even greater rates for protection. As a result of over crowding, pestilence breaks out among the people. Huge populations die. The Undead grow stronger. Even without invading armies of dead, whole cities of living creatures are replaced by the walking dead. Most crops are destroyed by pestilence as well.

The Azrac Empire trades with the Blessed Continent for obscene profits, thus bolstering the Empire's sagging defenses and economy. Though never that significant in the battle against the Undead, they do manage to hold their own and continue to profit from heavy trading throughout the next decade.

1145 LIR: Undead continue to take Alliance holdings. The Humans pull back to their strongholds closest to the Valley of Wonders, and cease their expansions, but they too begin to lose footage against the Undead onslaught.

1146 LIR: After a year in which the Valley teetered on the brink of oblivion, the High Men arrive in glory and power. Within a month, they stop the Undead advance. Together with the Alliance and the Humans, the High Men begin to win battles.

1148 LIR: After another harsh winter, the Frostlings begin to move into more central regions, as the Undead begin to scatter from High Men attacks. Many remote areas are washed with the chaos of battle, giving the Frostlings the perfect opportunity to claim large tracts of abandoned territory.

1149 LIR: The Undead are driven back to retreat into the shadows.

1152 LIR: The High Men disappear again, leaving their holdings empty. Only a few potent High Men remain to guard certain nodes of destructive potential. Most races scramble to snatch up their holdings and build upon them. This results in another conflict.

1159 LIR: With the High Men mostly gone, the Undead try to revisit their destruction upon the land, but the alliance is too strong, and after half a century of fighting, the Undead are simply too weak. The Undead change their plan of attack to one far more subtle—they start to work upon Meandor's mind.

1164 LIR: The Cult agrees to a number of non-aggression treaties with the Undead. Necromancers begin to hold influence among the Cult of Storms.

1172 LIR: High Men are spotted among certain Human settlements, but nothing comes of Keeper attempts to forge alliances.

1194 LIR: Meandor allies with the Goblins and begins scheming.

1197 LIR: A famine consumes the land for the next four years. Some races raid other races for food. The Halflings become quite rich from a trade compact with the Frostlings, whose land blossoms in the scorching heat of the drought. The Azracs, on the other hand, are forced to eat many of their stores, and their plans for another organized invasion of the Blessed Continent are scrapped.

1203 LIR: Frostling and Halfling relations chill. The deterioration of diplomacy causes a number of conflicts between the two races.

1204 LIR: After a decisive victory against the Orcs, driving the grunting race back to their caves and out of all surface holdings, Julia is promoted to lead the Keepers.

1206 LIR: The 'Decade of Silence' begins. (The next ten years are a time of uncertain peace, and no serious battles are fought during this time period. But instead of enjoying prosperity, there is a vast expansion in arms, as though a war is inevitable.)

1216 LIR: The Star appears over the Valley of Wonders... Meandor is seen creeping about the central Court Ruins, sifting through the bones of the dead. The Silence ends.

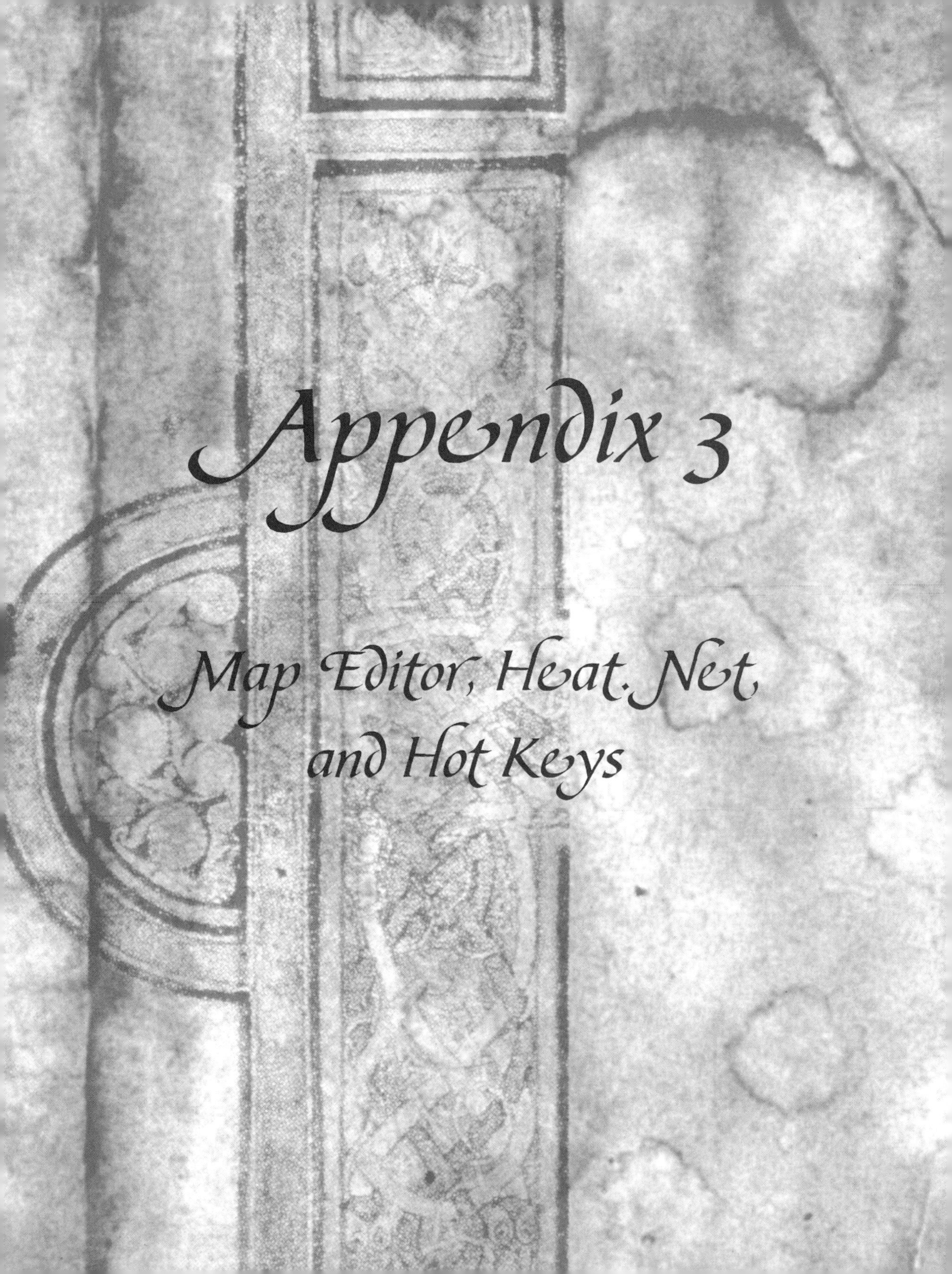

Appendix 3

Map Editor, Heat.Net and Hot Keys

Hot Keys

Arrow keys	*Scroll the map*
PGUP	*Map level up*
PGDN	*Map level down*
N or '.'	*Select next unit/army*
P or ','	*Select prev. unit/army*
H	*Select next Hero*
L	*Select leader*
D	*Select party as 'Done' for the current turn.*
G	*Guard On/Off*
C	*Center on selected unit/army*
CTRL-ENTER	*End Turn*
F2 or CTRL-O	*Open/Load game*
F3 or CTRL-S	*Save game*
M	*Move unit*
O	*Observe enemy movement*
SHIFT	*Hold SHIFT to select multiple parties or units for a single move command.*
ALT-ENTER	*Switches between full screen and Window display modes*
ESC	*Quits from most screens*
F1	*Recalls last tip in the Tutorial*

Play Over Heat.Net

SegaSoft's HEAT.NET Internet gaming service offers fast, free, online gaming. With dozens of dedicated servers across the United States, players can easily play *Age of Wonders* across the Internet. HEAT.NET features automatic "matchmaking" – where players are automatically connected to the fastest Internet servers for their Internet Service Provider (ISP).

To play on HEAT.NET, you will need a Java based web browser (such as Netscape or Internet Explorer 3.0+) and the HEAT client software, which is provided on the *Age of Wonders* CD-ROM. You will also need to create a free account on HEAT.NET. Note: You do not have to pay to play *Age of Wonders* on HEAT.NET.

The quickest way to get to the *Age of Wonders* game lobby on HEAT.NET, is to chose the HEAT.NET shortcut from your *Age of Wonders* Start Menu. Once selected, your default web browser will open to the *Age of Wonders* Direct Launch page. Then follow this procedure:

1. Be certain that the name of the game listed in the drop down menu is "*Age of Wonders*".
2. Type in your HEAT user name and password where prompted.
3. Click the "PLAY NOW" button.

Once the HEAT software loads, you will be brought immediately to the *Age of Wonders* main lobby. Here, you can chat with other people, create a new game room or join an existing game in progress.

For more assistance with HEAT.NET, log into http://www.heat.net, and select "HELP" from the top menu bar.

For up-to-date, specific information about *Age of Wonders* on HEAT.NET, go to the "*Age of Wonders* Game Page" on HEAT.NET by logging into http://www.heat.net, and choosing "GAMES" from the top menu then choose the "ACTION" channel. Locate the "*Age of Wonders*" link from the game list to the left.

Using the Age of Wonders Editor

Age of Wonders ships with a powerful scenario creation utility, AoWED. With this tool you'll be able to make your own AoW maps, and design heroes and items. Before attempting to use this utility, you should have a complete understanding of the game; it's difficult enough to create an entertaining, balanced map even after you've mastered the game itself.

Creating a new Scenario

When you first open up the *Age of Wonders* Editor, click File, then New. You will be presented with a dialogue box requesting details about the size of your new map:

Map size: Maps can range anywhere from Small (48x48 hex) to Extra Large (128x128 hex).

Map levels: Choose whether you want a surface-only map, or include one or both subterranean levels.

Choose your size according to the number of players you plan on including in the scenario. Small maps are best suited for one on one matches, while Extra Large maps can accommodate all 12 races.

Once you have chosen a map size, the editor will ask you for details about the map. Under the 'General' tab, enter the map's name and description, and choose which songs you'd like played in the background. You also have the option of requiring a password in order to edit the map. (Useful for keeping your pesky friends from ruining your work)

The next tab, Settings, allows you to decide who will inhabit your map, as well as what defines winning. In the Restrictions box, you choose how many players will be on the map, how many magic spheres they may choose, and the number of heroes each player may control. If you wish to include any special victory conditions, you may do so in the aptly named box. Next, you may choose which races are allowed in the scenario, as well as the personality of the Independents.

The third tab, Players, allows you to define the specifics for each player. In the 'Player' box, choose which player you'd like to edit. In the successive boxes, you may choose which race this player controls, whether they are played by a human player or the computer (Check the 'fixed' box to force this choice), and the behavior of the player if it is computer-controlled. Below this, you may define the amount of gold and mana the player begins with, as well as the amount of external (free) gold and mana that player receives each turn. Finally, you may enter an objective to guide the player to victory. Be sure to fill this tab out for each player.

Diplomacy, the final tab, allows you to decide the initial relations between the players included in the scenario. Click on the question marks to cycle through the four options: Unknown, Peace, War, and Alliance.

Once you are satisfied with all the options, click 'OK' to begin creating your world.

The Editor Interface

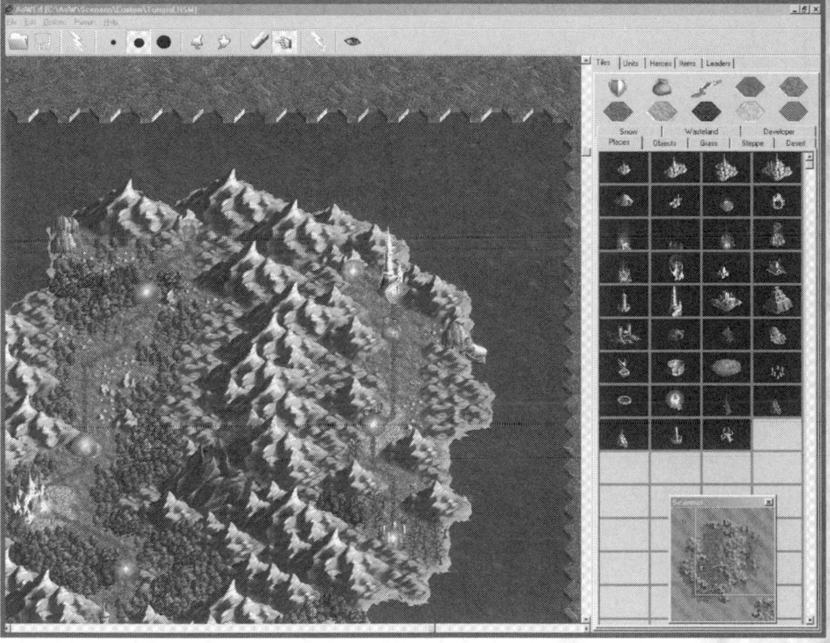

The top row of icons, allows you to do several things. The first two icons are Open and Save, respectively. The third icon, Validate, will verify that the map will play correctly. The next three icons represent the size of the brush used to add terrain to the map. The two icons following allow you to switch between the surface and underground layers (if you chose to include them in your map). Next come the Eraser and Select Object icons, which are used to remove or select objects such as trees and mountains from. The Overwrite Terrain icon allows terrain to be, well, overwritten. The final icon, Preview Mode, will switch to the game-engine view of the map.

The largest portion of the screen, along the left-hand side, is the map window. Through this window you can view and interact with your creation. The small 'Scanner' floater contains a small map of the world. The right-hand side of the screen contains the various items available for inclusion in the scenario. The Tiles tab contains the groundwork of your map — terrain, party, item, and town placement is all done from this tab.

Begin by selecting a terrain (click on the 'Grass' tab underneath the 'Tiles' tab, for instance) and type (click on a mountain). Now click anywhere in the main map window. You can deselect the mountain by right clicking, or by choosing another item type. Choose the green hex icon near the top right of the screen; these seven terrain hex icons represent basic terrain placement of each type of terrain (Water, Grass, Steppe, Desert, Wasteland, Snow, and Ice). Now click a few times around your mountain, surrounding it with grass.

Next, click on the 'Places' tab. Select a city of any size, and place it on the grass near your mountain. The city initially shows up with a large **?** covering it, as you haven't provided any specific information about it yet. Let's do that now. Right click anywhere to deselect the 'place city' cursor, and then right click on the placed city. Click once on the city, then right click it. A menu will pop up; choose 'Edit.' On this menu, you may name the city, and choose its starting conditions: who controls it, which race inhabits it, whether it has a wall and defenders, and what upgrade level it has reached.

Now place some more terrain, covering the map as you like. Add a few more cities, and a few power nodes and farms as well. (Both are available on the Tiles/Places tab.) You can use the Road icon (Located on the top right of the screen, near the Terrain hex icons) to connect your towns. If you wish, you may place parties of units on the map by clicking the Party icon (Also on the top right, represented by a shield). Choose a place on the map for the party to go, and click. Two floaters will appear. On the Army Properties floater, choose which player will control the party, what behavior the party will follow (for AI players), and the direction the party faces. On the Unit floater, you may choose any unit or hero to include in the party by clicking its portrait, then hitting 'Add' on the Army Properties floater. When you are finished, click 'OK.'

The final icon on the Tiles tab is the Item icon. (Represented by a bag, just to the right of the Party icon) Choose the Unit icon, and then click on the map somewhere. Two more floaters arise. You have the option of allowing the computer to randomly place items of a certain value, or you may choose the items yourself. Let's place some Dragon Scale Armor. In the Item floater, click on the Dragon Scale Armor, then click 'Add' in the item bag properties. Click 'OK,' and the armor will be placed on the map.

Now that you are familiar with the Tiles tab, click the next tab, 'Units.' From here you may view all units in the game, and you can place units on the map by first selecting the unit, then clicking on the map. You can create parties this way as well; simply place several units on the same hex, then select the party of units and right click to edit its properties.

The third main tab, Heroes, allows you to place heroes on the map. It works very similarly to the Units tab, although you can create your own heroes as well! (By clicking on the 'Add Hero' icon)

The fourth tab, Items, follows the same pattern as the earlier tabs. You can place items by selecting the item, and then placing it on the map, and you can create your own items.

Finally, we have the Leaders tab. Here you can place the leaders of each player onto the map. Once you have placed the leader, you may edit its properties if you wish: click on it, then right click and choose 'Edit.' The Army Properties floater will pop up, and you can then select the leader and choose 'Edit.'

You now know the basics of map creation. In order to be successful in designing maps, you should begin with a rough outline of the map, including major cities and locations, and then continue to add niceties to your map such as trees and hills to add realism. Always be sure to play test the map a LOT! Play all sides, and ensure that each player has an equal opportunity to achieve victory. Have fun creating your own worlds!

Troubleshooting

Game boots to a black screen–

Try playing the game in a Window. If the game runs in a window but not full screen, make sure you have the latest version of DirectX installed or download new video drivers for your video card. If the screen turns black or distorted after a resolution switch try turning off "Auto Res Switching.î This will display the game at a fixed resolution and display scenes like the intro and setup screen boxed when the game is set to run in resolutions higher than 640x480.

Game crashes at startup or won't boot–

In the AoW setup program, check the 'Skip Intro' box, and verify that the ìUse DirectSoundî box is unchecked. If the game runs, there may be some incompatibilities with your Windows media drivers for video playing, and/or DirectSound drivers. Try updating your DirectX drivers.

No sound–

Try toggling "DirectSound" off/on in the game or with the AoW Setup program. Make sure you have the latest version of DirectX installed.

Game runs slowly–

Low-end systems (sub P2s) should run the game in the lowest resolution: 640x480. If the game is still slow, run the game in the lowest detail level (you will only lose some transparency effects). Decreasing the sound quality or turning off sound altogether will also speed up the game.

Mouse Movement is slow–

The mouse movement is linked to the game's frame rate - on slower machines the mouse will move slower as well. Try running the game in a lower resolution and/or decreasing detail level using the AoW Setup program.

Tech Support

Having a problem getting your game to run? Problems with DirectX? Sound kind of nonexistent? Please check out the file readme.txt on the CD for last minute information and answers to frequently asked questions (FAQs).

Do you want to ask a specific technical question? You can e-mail us directly at:

Support@godgames.com

If you would prefer to talk to someone in person, you can reach our tech support staff at (214) 303-1202. Our hours of operation are seven days a week from 9 a.m. to 9 p.m. Central Time.

If you prefer U.S. mail, please use the following address:

Gathering of Developers
P.O. Box 565032
Dallas, TX 75356
Attn: Tech Support

Credits

Triumph Studios and Epic Games

Designer and Director . . . . . .Lennart Sas
Additional Design . . .Arno van Wingerden
Lead Programmer . .Arno van Wingerden
Programmer . . . . .Josh Farley
Artists . . . . .Lennart Sas
Thomas Cardin
Roy Postma
Lead Scenario Designer . . . . . .Menno Sas
Scenario Designers . . . . .Doug Gibson
Arnout Sas
Hugo van Wingerden
Writer . . . . .Raymond Bingham
Music . . . . .Michiel van den Bos
Sound FX . . . . .Nando Eweg
Galaxy Sound System . . .Carlo Vogelsang
Internet Mail Suite .Argo Software Design
Bizz . . . . .Jay Wilbur
Mark Rein
QA Core . . . . .Cliff Benjamin
Ian Calderon
Ted Stephenson
Hugo van Wingerden
Special Thanks . . . . .Eelco van der Snoek
Dietmer Tan
Arjan Brussee
Daniel Cook

Gathering of Developers

CEO . . . . .Mike Wilson
President and COO . . . . .Harry Miller
VP of Marketing . . . . .Jim Bloom
CFO . . . . .Rick Stults
Corporate Development . . . . .Binu Philip
Director of Media . . . . .Doug Myres
Sales . . . . .David Gershik
Operations . . . . .Terry Nagy
Administrative . . . . . .Joanna Carr-Brown
Online Support . . . . .Tempest Digital
Concrete Support . . . . .Rich Vos
Jason Birdwell
Kyle Hlavenka
Shane Love
Mike Holcombe
Jerrod Lai

Manual Creation

Authorship . . . . .Stratos Group
Raymond Bingham
Design and Printing . . . . . .Mars Publishing

Index

Age of Wonders

Limited Software Warranty and License Agreement

This LIMITED SOFTWARE WARRANTY AND LICENSE AGREEMENT (this "Agreement"), including the Limited Warranty and other special provisions, is a legal agreement between You (either an individual or an entity) and Triumph Software and Gathering of Developers I, Ltd., (collectively, the "Owner") regarding this software product and the materials contained therein and related thereto. Your act of installing and/or otherwise using the software constitutes Your agreement to be bound by the terms of this Agreement. If You do not agree to the terms of this Agreement, promptly return the software packaging and the accompanying materials (including any hardware, manuals, other written materials and packaging) to the place You obtained them, along with your receipt, for a full refund.

Grant of Limited Non-Exclusive License. This Agreement permits You to use one (1) copy of the software program(s) (the "SOFTWARE") included in this package for your personal use on a single home or portable computer. The SOFTWARE is in "use" on a computer when it is loaded into temporary memory (i.e., RAM) or installed into the permanent memory (e.g., hard disk, CD-ROM, or other storage device) of that computer. Installation on a network server is strictly prohibited, except under a special and separate network license obtained from Owner; this Agreement shall not serve as such necessary special network license. Installation on a network server constitutes "use" that must comply with the terms of this Agreement. This license is not a sale of the original SOFTWARE or any copy thereof.

Intellectual Property Ownership. Owner retains all right, title and interest to this SOFTWARE and the accompanying manual(s), packaging and other written materials (collectively, the "ACCOMPANYING MATERIALS"), including, but not limited to, all copyrights, trademarks, trade secrets, trade names, proprietary rights, patents, titles, computer codes, audiovisual effects, themes, characters, character names, stories, dialog, settings, artwork, sounds effects, musical works, and moral rights. The SOFTWARE and ACCOMPANYING MATERIALS are protected by United States copyright law and applicable copyright laws and treaties throughout the World. All rights are reserved. The SOFTWARE and ACCOMPANYING MATERIALS may not be copied or reproduced in any manner or medium, in whole or in part, without prior written consent from Owner. Any persons copying or reproducing all or any portion of the SOFTWARE or ACCOMPANYING MATERIALS, in any manner or medium, will be willfully violating the copyright laws and may be subject to civil or criminal penalties.

SOFTWARE Backup or Archiving. After You install the SOFTWARE into the permanent memory of a computer, You may keep and use the original disk(s) and/or CD-ROM (the "Storage Media") only for backup or archival purposes.

Restrictions. Other than as provided specifically in this Agreement, You are not permitted to copy or otherwise reproduce the SOFTWARE or ACCOMPANYING MATERIALS; modify or prepare derivative copies based on the SOFTWARE or ACCOMPANYING MATERIALS; distribute copies of the SOFTWARE or ACCOMPANYING MATERIALS by sale or other transfer of ownership; rent, lease, or lend the SOFTWARE or ACCOMPANYING MATERIALS; or to display the SOFTWARE or ACCOMPANYING MATERIALS publicly. You are expressly prohibited from transmitting the SOFTWARE or ACCOMPANYING MATERIALS electronically or otherwise over the Internet or through any other media or to any other party. You are expressly prohibited from using or selling any unauthorized level packs, add-on packs or sequels based upon or related to the SOFTWARE or ACCOMPANYING MATERIALS. You are expressly prohibited from selling or using any characters or other components of the game for any purpose. You are expressly prohibited from selling or otherwise profiting from any levels, add-on packs, sequels or other items created by utilization of the SOFTWARE's level editor. YOU ARE NOT PERMITTED TO REVERSE ENGINEER, DECOMPILE OR DISASSEMBLE THE SOFTWARE IN ANY WAY. Any copying of the SOFTWARE or ACCOMPANYING MATERIALS not specifically allowed in this Agreement is a violation of this Agreement.

Limited Warranty and Warranty Disclaimers.

LIMITED WARRANTY. Owner warrants that the original Storage Media holding the SOFTWARE is free from defects in materials and workmanship under normal use and service for a period of ninety (90) days from the date of purchase as evidenced by Your receipt. If for any reason You find defects in the Storage Media, or if you are unable to install the SOFTWARE on your home or portable computer, You may return the SOFTWARE and all ACCOMPANYING MATERIALS to the place You obtained it for a full refund. This limited warranty does not apply if You have damaged the SOFTWARE by accident or abuse.

CUSTOMER'S REMEDY. Your exclusive remedies, and the entire liability of Owner, shall be (i) replacement of any original Storage Media with the SOFTWARE or (ii) full refund of the price paid for this SOFTWARE. By opening the sealed software packaging, installing and/or otherwise using the SOFTWARE or ACCOMPANYING MATERIALS, you hereby agree to waive any and all other remedies you may have at law or in equity. Any such remedies you may not waive as a matter of public policy, you hereby assign, or shall assign as they become available, over to Owner.

WARRANTY DISCLAIMERS. EXCEPT FOR THE EXPRESS LIMITED WARRANTY SET FORTH ABOVE, OWNER MAKES NO WARRANTIES, EXPRESS OR IMPLIED, ORAL OR WRITTEN, CONCERNING THE PRODUCTS OR ANY COMPONENT PART THEREOF. ANY IMPLIED WARRANTIES THAT MAY BE IMPOSED BY APPLICABLE LAW ARE LIMITED IN ALL RESPECTS TO THE FULLEST EXTENT ALLOWED AND TO THE DURATION OF THE LIMITED WARRANTY. OWNER DOES NOT REPRESENT, WARRANT OR GUARANTEE THE QUALITY OR THE PERFORMANCE OF THE SOFTWARE OR ACCOMPANYING MATERIALS OTHER THAN AS SET FORTH IN THE ABOVE LIMITED WARRANTY. OWNER ALSO DOES NOT REPRESENT, WARRANT OR GUARANTEE THAT THE SOFTWARE OR ACCOMPANYING MATERIALS' CAPABILITIES WILL MEET YOUR NEEDS OR THAT THE SOFTWARE WILL CONTINUOUSLY OPERATE, BE ERROR FREE, OR THAT PROBLEMS WILL BE CORRECTED. OWNER DOES NOT REPRESENT THAT THE SOFTWARE WILL OPERATE IN A MULTI-USER ENVIRONMENT.

NO ORAL OR WRITTEN INFORMATION OR ADVICE GIVEN BY OWNER, ITS DEALERS, DISTRIBUTORS, DIRECTORS, OFFICERS, EMPLOYEES, AGENTS, CONTRACTORS OR AFFILIATES SHALL CREATE ANY OTHER WARRANTY OR EXTEND OR EXPAND THE SCOPE OF THIS WARRANTY. YOU MAY NOT RELY ON ANY SUCH INFORMATION OR ADVICE.

SOME STATES DO NOT ALLOW LIMITATIONS ON HOW LONG AN IMPLIED WARRANTY LASTS, SO THE ABOVE LIMITATION MAY NOT APPLY TO YOU. THIS LIMITED WARRANTY GIVES YOU SPECIFIC LEGAL RIGHTS AND YOU MAY ALSO HAVE OTHER RIGHTS WHICH MAY VARY FROM STATE TO STATE.

LIABILITY LIMITATION. To the maximum extent permitted by applicable law, and regardless of whether any remedy set forth herein fails of its essential purpose, IN NO EVENT WILL OWNER, ITS DIRECTORS, OFFICERS, EMPLOYEES, AGENTS OR AFFILIATES NOR ANYONE ELSE INVOLVED IN THE DEVELOPMENT, MANUFACTURE OR DISTRIBUTION OF THE SOFTWARE OR THE ACCOMPANYING MATERIALS BE LIABLE FOR ANY DAMAGES WHATSOEVER, INCLUDING WITHOUT LIMITATION, DIRECT OR INDIRECT; INCIDENTAL; OR CONSEQUENTIAL DAMAGES FOR PERSONAL INJURY, PERSONAL PROPERTY, LOSS OF BUSINESS PROFITS, BUSINESS INTERRUPTION, LOSS OF BUSINESS INFORMATION, LOSS OF TEXT OR DATA STORED IN OR USED WITH THE SOFTWARE INCLUDING THE COST OF RECOVERING OR REPRODUCING THE TEXT OR DATA, OR ANY OTHER PECUNIARY LOSS, ARISING FROM OR OUT OF THE USE OR INABILITY TO USE THIS SOFTWARE. THIS LIABILITY LIMITATION APPLIES EVEN IF YOU OR ANYONE ELSE HAS ADVISED OWNER OR ANY OF ITS AUTHORIZED REPRESENTATIVES OF THE POSSIBILITY OF SUCH DAMAGES. EVEN IF SUCH IS CAUSED BY, ARISES OUT OF OR RESULTS FROM THE ORDINARY, STRICT, SOLE OR CONTRIBUTORY NEGLIGENCE OF OWNER OR ITS DIRECTORS, OFFICERS, EMPLOYEES, AGENTS, CONTRACTORS OR AFFILIATES. SOME STATES DO NOT ALLOW THE EXCLUSION OR LIMITATION OF INCIDENTAL OR CONSEQUENTIAL DAMAGES, SO THE ABOVE LIMITATION OR EXCLUSION MAY NOT APPLY TO YOU.

Product Support and Updates. This SOFTWARE is intended to be user-friendly and limited product support is provided by Owner as specified in the ACCOMPANYING MATERIALS.

Jurisdiction. TEXAS LAWS GOVERN THIS AGREEMENT, REGARDLESS OF EACH STATE'S CHOICE OF LAW PRINCIPLES, WITH A FORUM AND VENUE OF DALLAS COUNTY, TEXAS. This Agreement may be modified only by a written instrument specifying the modification and executed by both parties. In the event that any provision of this Agreement shall be held to be unenforceable, such provision shall be enforced to the greatest possible extent, with the other provisions of this Agreement to remain in full force and effect.

Entire Agreement. This Agreement represents the entire agreement between the parties, and supersedes any oral or written communications, proposals or prior agreements between the parties or any dealers, distributors, agents or employees.

U.S. Government Restricted Rights. The SOFTWARE and the ACCOMPANYING MATERIALS is provided with RESTRICTED RIGHTS (as found in 48 C.F.R. §52.227-7013). This provision only applies if the U.S. Government or any of its entities obtains this SOFTWARE either directly or indirectly. Owner created this SOFTWARE and the ACCOMPANYING MATERIALS exclusively with private funds. Additionally, information contained in this SOFTWARE and the ACCOMPANYING MATERIALS is a trade secret of Owner for all purposes of the Freedom of Information Act or otherwise. Furthermore, this SOFTWARE is "commercial computer software" subject to limited use as set forth in any contract that may be entered into between the seller and the governmental entity. Owner owns, in all respects, the proprietary information and proprietary data found in the SOFTWARE and the ACCOMPANYING MATERIALS.

U.S. DEPARTMENT OF DEFENSE PERSONNEL. Owner only sells this SOFTWARE and the ACCOMPANYING MATERIALS with "Restricted Rights" as defined in DFARS 52.227-7013 (also found at 48 C.F.R. §252.227-7013). Any U.S. Government use, duplication, or disclosure is subject to the restrictions including, but not limited to those found in the Rights in Technological Data clause at DFARS 52.227-7013 (48 C.F.R. §252.227-7013) that may be amended from time to time.

NON-DEPARTMENT OF DEFENSE PERSONNEL. Other governmental personnel are on notice through this Agreement that any use of this SOFTWARE and the ACCOMPANYING MATERIALS is subject to similar limitations as those stated above, including but not limited to, those stated in Commercial Computer SOFTWARE — Restricted Rights found in 48 C.F.R. §52.227-19, that may also be amended from time to time. Manufacturer is Owner at the location listed below.

U.S. Export Laws Prohibitions. By opening the sealed software packaging and/or installing or otherwise using the SOFTWARE and ACCOMPANYING MATERIALS, You also agree and confirm that the SOFTWARE or ACCOMPANYING MATERIALS and any of the SOFTWARE's direct products are not being and will not be transported, exported or re-exported (directly or indirectly through the Internet or otherwise) into (or to a national or resident of) any country forbidden to receive such SOFTWARE or ACCOMPANYING MATERIALS by any U.S. export laws or accompanying regulations or otherwise violate such laws or regulations, that may be amended from time to time. You also agree and confirm that the SOFTWARE and ACCOMPANYING MATERIALS will not be used for any purpose that may be restricted by the same laws and regulations.

Termination. This Agreement is valid until terminated. This Agreement ceases automatically (without any form of notice) if You do not comply with any Agreement provision. You can also end this Agreement by destroying the SOFTWARE and ACCOMPANYING MATERIALS and all copies and reproductions of the SOFTWARE and ACCOMPANYING MATERIALS and deleting and permanently purging the SOFTWARE from any client server or computer on which it has been installed.

Program Transfer. You may permanently transfer all of your rights under this Agreement, provided that the recipient agrees to all of the terms of this Agreement, and You agree to transfer all ACCOMPANYING MATERIALS and related documents and components and remove the SOFTWARE from Your computer prior. Transferring the SOFTWARE automatically terminates Your license under this Agreement.

Equitable Remedies You hereby agree that if the terms of this Agreement are not specifically enforced, Owner will be irreparably damaged, and therefore you agree that Owner shall be entitled, without bond, other security, proof of damages, to appropriate equitable remedies with respect any of this Agreement, in addition to any other available remedies.Owner If You have any questions regarding this Agreement, the enclosed materials, or otherwise, please contact in writing:

Gathering of Developers
2700 Fairmount Street
Dallas, Texas 75201
Attn: Customer Service